Cambridge Proficiency

Examination Practice 1

Teacher's Book

Edited by Leo Jones for the University of Cambridge Local Examinations Syndicate

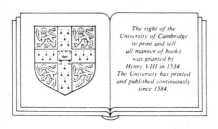

The right of the
University of Cambridge
to print and sell
all manner of books
was granted by
Henry VIII in 1534.
The University has printed
and published continuously
since 1584.

Cambridge University Press
Cambridge
New York   Port Chester
Melbourne   Sydney

GW00374469

Published by the Press Syndicate of the University of Cambridge
The Pitt Building, Trumpington Street, Cambridge CB2 1RP
40 West 20th Street, New York, NY 10011–4211, USA
10 Stamford Road, Oakleigh, Melbourne 3166, Australia

© Cambridge University Press 1984

First published 1984
Tenth printing 1991

Printed in Great Britain
by J. W. Arrowsmith Ltd, Bristol

ISBN 0 521 27426 5 Teacher's Book
ISBN 0 521 27425 7 Student's Book
ISBN 0 521 26356 5 Set of 2 cassettes

HE

Contents

Thanks

Thanks are due to the many collaborators who contributed to these materials and in particular to Richard Alderson, Lois Arthur, Sheila Condon, John Cowley, Frank Chaplen, Heather Daldry, Diana Fried-Booth, Patrick Gribben, Kathy Gude, Louise Hashemi, Tony Hopwood, Christian Kay, Roy Kingsbury, Ivor Levinson, Susan Morris, S. O'Connell, Raymond Pinder, Christopher Ross, Roger Scott, Alan Stanton, Wendy Stott, Jeff Stranks, Vivienne Ward, Pauline Werba, and to the Test Development and Research Unit.

Publisher's note
For details of sources of illustrations and other copyright material please see the Student's Book.

Introduction

The tests in *Cambridge Proficiency Examination Practice* are designed to familiarise students with the style and format of the Certificate of Proficiency in English (CPE) examination papers and to provide them with practice in examination techniques. The tests can be used in class for pre-examination practice and discussion, as 'mock examinations', or by students working alone using the Teacher's Book as a key. The tests are reproduced exactly as they will appear in the modified examination, reflecting the new size and layout of the exam paper.

A suggested marking scheme for each of the tests is provided in the Teacher's Book, but it must be emphasised that no fully authoritative assessment of students can be based on this. In the CPE examination itself a series of complex statistical procedures is carried out to correlate a candidate's performance in all five papers, and such procedures cannot be accurately reproduced by the teacher working alone.

A number of changes have been made in the CPE examination syllabus for 1984. Broadly speaking, there are four different ideas underlying the changes in the syllabus:

a) the now universal acceptance of communicative approaches in the EFL classroom, which should be reflected in and, indeed, encouraged by the CPE examination;
b) the increased prominence of listening and speaking skills in classrooms, reflected in greater weighting in the examination;
c) the view that reading and listening texts should be taken from authentic sources within a candidate's range of experience, and not be specially written, abridged or over-literary;
d) the need to avoid culture bias in the examination, confirming the status of English as an international language.

The ways in which these ideas are embodied in the examination itself are outlined on pages 2 to 14 and can be seen in the practice tests in the Student's Book.

The five complete tests in *Cambridge Proficiency Examination Practice 1* include specimen material previously issued by the Syndicate (*Changes of Syllabus in 1984*) and four more tests consisting of material taken from the Syndicate's bank of material or specially adapted from the examinations of 1981–3.

The Teacher's Book contains:
– a suggested marking scheme and answer key for each paper;
– complete transcripts of the recorded Listening Comprehension tests;
– instructions on the handling of the Interview tests.

The two accompanying Cassettes contain the recordings for the Listening Comprehension tests. The tests cannot be used without the appropriate cassette.

The Certificate of Proficiency Examination

The chart below gives an outline of how each paper of the CPE examination is assessed. In the examination the final assessment of any candidate is reached only on the basis of total performance in all five papers and after the marks have been carefully adjusted to establish correct weightings and grading levels. Adjustments are also made to offset the effect of random guessing in multiple-choice and true / false questions. Since such procedures are clearly impracticable for the teacher working alone, the marks shown below and throughout the Teacher's Book should be treated as a guide and not as official 'pass marks'. The 'raw' marks for each paper are in any case subject to adjustment / weighting to bring them to the totals shown below.

The complete examination carries a total of 180 marks.

Name of paper	Time	Total marks	Assessment
Paper 1 Reading Comprehension	1 hour	40	On average, pass candidates will score a total of about 24, good candidates about 30 and very good candidates about 36.
Paper 2 Composition	2 hours	40	An impression mark is given, following a grading scale for each composition. On average, pass candidates score a paper total of about 16, good candidates about 24 and very good candidates about 32 or more.
Paper 3 Use of English	2 hours	40	This paper is marked according to a detailed marking scheme. On average, pass candidates score 20 to 24.
Paper 4 Listening Comprehension	about 30 minutes	20	This paper is marked according to a detailed marking scheme with varied weighting for items. On average, pass candidates score about 12 marks.
Paper 5 Interview	about 15 minutes	40	An impression mark is given for each section, following grading scales. On average, pass candidates score about 24.

A pass candidate might score a final total of about 100, a good candidate about 125 and a very good candidate about 150 out of a possible maximum of 180 marks.

Paper 1: Reading Comprehension (1 hour)

Paper 1 is in two sections: Section A with 25 multiple-choice questions, each consisting of a sentence with a blank to be filled by one of four words or phrases, and Section B with 15 multiple-choice questions on three or more reading passages. (This represents a change from the paper as set up to 1983, which contained 40 five-choice items in Section A and 20 four-choice items in Section B with a time allowance of 1¼ hours.)

Section A tests candidates' knowledge of English vocabulary (including synonyms, antonyms, collocations and phrasal verbs) as well as their knowledge of grammatical rules and constraints. (This represents an increased emphasis on grammar and usage as compared with the 1983 examination.)

Section B tests candidates' general understanding of the gist of passages as well as their understanding of specific information given. Some questions also test appreciation of stylistic effects, nuance and register. The passages vary in length, character and density and are drawn from a variety of authentic sources, including fiction, non-fiction, newspapers, magazines, brochures, leaflets and advertisements.

Marking

Section A carries a total possible mark of 25; the 15 questions in Section B count **double**, giving a final total (scaled to 40) of 55. A score representing a pass in this paper is thus about 33 out of 55 (i.e. 24 marks out of the scaled total of 40).

Exam preparation

It is important not to practise this type of test to excess, but merely to accustom students to its requirements and tempo. Multiple-choice questions have more value as a testing device than as a teaching method and excessive practice in doing this type of test is unlikely to improve students' ability to read English more efficiently. Time should be devoted in class, therefore, to improving students' reading skills and not just their ability to answer reading comprehension questions.

Students should be given experience of reading authentic texts of the kind shown in *Cambridge Proficiency Examination Practice 1* and given help in learning how to understand them. Such help may include teaching students how to understand the gist of a passage and how to extract the main points of information from it without necessarily understanding every single word they read.

Paper 2: Composition (2 hours)

Two compositions, of the varying word length specified, are to be written in the 2 hours allotted. (Up to 1983 the paper required two compositions, from a choice of two descriptive and two discursive topics, and a comprehension / appreciation exercise, with a time allowance of three hours.)

The choice of topics includes (at the full 350-word length) a descriptive and a discursive topic, a shorter more specific topic or an exercise based on a specific task (normally of about 200 words) and a topic (of 350 words) based on optional reading as specified in the examination Regulations for each year. The advantage for candidates of choosing to read one of the three texts selected for the exam is that it may offer them an enjoyable and worthwhile reading experience, with an opportunity to develop the ability to handle ideas and literary themes in English, as well as a wider range of topics to choose from in Paper 2. Candidates may also have the chance to discuss their reading in the Interview (see page 13).

Marking

An impression mark out of 20 is given for each composition, using the scale shown below. This mark is based on an overall impression of the language used, including the range and appropriateness of vocabulary, sentence and paragraph structure and correctness of grammar, spelling and punctuation. Individual mistakes are not penalised. The language used should be, for a pass grade and above, at a level of fluency, accuracy and resource appropriate to the Proficiency examination, reflected also in the relevance and organisation of each composition as a whole and in terms of individual preparation.

In topics 1 to 3 language rather than content is the main concern since a candidate's general command of the language shows in the attempt to communicate some personal interest in the topic. Marks are not taken off for unorthodox opinions, illogical arguments or lack of special creativity in selecting and developing descriptive detail.

The task-directed exercise is intended to reveal sensitivity to features of style appropriate to the English used for various special purposes, and ability to reproduce these features appropriately.

The topics on the three books are also task-directed, in the sense that they require ability to recall and marshal facts and themes from the text studied in the framework of the question set. Detailed factual recall is not a crucial factor in the marking, nor is training in the technique of literary analysis, the emphasis being, as with the other topics, on the quality of language used in response to the given stimulus.

For all topics, the inclusion of irrelevant material which seems to have been learnt by heart does lose marks. Over-short compositions will lose marks, as may over-long ones, because they often contain more mistakes or are badly structured. Pass candidates score about 8 for each composition, good candidates about 12 and very good candidates about 16. The chart below shows the scale used to assess each composition.

| 18–20 | Excellent | Error-free, substantial and varied material, resourceful and controlled in language and expression. |
| 16–17 | Very Good | Good realisation of task, ambitious and natural in style. |

4

12–15	Good	Sufficient assurance and freedom from basic error to maintain theme.
8–11	Pass	Clear realisation of task, reasonably correct and natural.
5–7	Weak	Near to pass level in general scope, but with numerous errors or too elementary in style.
0–4	Very Poor	Basic errors, narrowness of vocabulary.

The following sample compositions taken from the Syndicate's reports illustrate the quality of language which typifies candidates in these six gradings.

EXCELLENT (20 marks)

Much has been said about Women's rights, equal opportunities for women and the triumph of the emancipated women of our day. Does this all mean that a woman's place is no longer in the home, that she now stands shoulder-to-shoulder with fellow men, and women, in the strife and struggle of carreer, profession or politics?

Let us make a brief examination of the role of women in the past. Woman, from the cave-dwelling days of the human race, has always been wife, mother and home-maker. Life-styles changed through the epochs of history, but the role of woman remained unquestioned till not too long ago.

Man, being physically stronger and more agressive, was hunter, protector, and later in history, breadwinner, while woman, the weaker sex, biologically handicapped by child-bearing and child-minding, busied herself in the home. Her duties, while requiring less physical exertion than man's, were no less important nor less difficult. The roles of man and women were different, but complementary.

What of the role of women in modern Society? As life-styles changed through the ages, man the hunter became man the farmer and later, with industrialization, the farmer was transformed to mere breadwinner. Woman of today finds herself capable of taking over a bread-winner's job. More over, she need no longer be protected by her men (father, brothers or husband) – she is protected by the law. These two drastic changes have brought about the change that has taken place in the thinking of women, and most men, today.

Woman is better educated now than ever before, and justly feels that she is the equal of all men. She is no longer satisfied with being confined to the drudgery of housework.

While it cannot be denied that a respectable profession or carreer is much more exciting than the routine of household chores, and that a man with a working wife is priviledged with an augmented household income, it must be stressed that it is the woman that makes a home.

The basic unit of society is the family. In its simplest form, the family consists of father, mother and children (or child). While the needs of the family in terms of food, clothing and other modern necessities have to be provided for, the needs of the children must not be neglected. By her very nature woman is more loving, caring and warm – she is gifted with the elements that make up a home-maker and child-minder. In these, she is better equipped than man. It is only logical that her place is in the home.

For all that has been said of the liberation of women, most people in society today are still aware of the importance of women in the home. How often have we heard of women combining carreer with marriage (the latter, needless to say, means home-making) How often too, have we read of highly successful women putting aside all professional matters to look after their children till they are independant. Surely we all know, consciously, or subconsciously, that equality is not synonymous with similarity!

VERY GOOD (17 marks)

Last year I decided to spend a weekend with a friend of mine. I prefer not to say his name. I don't know why; certainly not for shyness or embarassment. Perhaps the most suitable words are these of Bernard Shaw: "When I like people immensely I never tell their name. It is like surrendering a part of them".

As I said before, we decided to interrupt our studies for a short period of time and to go to the sea, where he had a little house. The weather was beautiful; the sky was blue; the rays of the sun coloured everything with a golden light; the waves broke gently on the smooth sand; the beach was unlittered and untrodden by any kind of steps. "In this atmosphere" I was always thinking by myself "nothing can go wrong".

What I remember about the first day is perfectly clear in my mind; I think I will never be able to forget that day. We went on boat to a small isle near the coast. It stood, just in front of us like an immense finger. The rocks laid just a little below the level of the sea; this fact made the navigation even of a small boat very difficult if you were not an expert of that place. All looked like a person you cannot trust in, all smiles outside but dangerous inside so that you do not recognise the danger until it is too late.

When the sun began to set and finally plunged into the deep infinity of the sea, we came back.

That evening was the most beautiful evening I've ever had. Now, while I am recalling it to my mind, it appears to me as something of fantastic, of strange. I don't remember shapes, appearances, figures, but only smells, voices, scents, sounds: the smell of his garments imbued with smoke, the voice of his heart, the scent of his strong perfume, the sound of the wind whistling among the trees.

Well, now you can ask yourself: "But that was a beautiful holiday!! Nothing went disastrously wrong".

I tell you in a minute. The day following I got up early and he was not there. I went out from the bedroom, wandering from one room to another: the house was desert. Outside there was a terrible storm; thumbers and lightenings were shacking the walls; the sky was monstrously dark; the sea was rough.

At least I found a letter in the kitchen. I opened it with mingled sentiments of fear and curiosity, and I read these words: "Please, forgive me".

GOOD (15 marks)

Jane Eyre is often described as a passionate caracter in the book, but she suffers an inner struggle. Her love for Mr Rochester is full of devotion, faith in him and truth. She is passionate and has a strong personality at the same time in the sense that her conscience is stronger than her desires. She wants to be a free human being with self-esteem, self-respect. She said herself that even if she has nobody in the world, is poor and plain she wants to preserve her self-seteem. Being Rochester's mistress would be an easy way to fulfill her desires, her love for Rochester, and she could not care for other people. But conscience acts as a tyrant on her. Conscience can be compared to a dictator who opresses her, emprisonnes her. Rochester even said to himself that if he assaulted her physically her mind would not resist. So we see the strong power of conscience over Jane. She suffers from this conduct that she decided to adopt, she feels frustrated, but at the same time this conscience is the only thing that she has got and it is very precious and important for her. It is her conscience which makes her leave Thornfield, Rochester. Jane's conscience contrasts with Rochester's irresponsability, and inconsciousness when he wants to marry her being already married. All through the novel we see this struggle between Jane's passion for Rochester and her conscience, and Rochester's love for Jane and his impulsivity. Jane does not want to be abandonned by Rochester in the same way he did with his other mistresses. Jane suffers from this conscience but this moral integrity makes her being respected from the others. She wants people to respect her as well as she respects them. Conscience is not only a tyrant for Jane Eyre because she heard Rochester by "the voice" of the conscience and she decided to answer to Rochester's call. She has a complete faith in conscience and God. We can see another problem of conscience in the book when St John wants to marry her, not because he loves her but because she could be a good helper as a missionary's wife in India. We see the contrast between St John and Rochester. The first one wanting to marry her without loving her, and Rochester wanting to be his mistress and loving. Jane said to St John that she could help people in England first without going so far to India. We can see the inner struggle in Jane Eyre's mind, and Rochester's voice will save her, this later conscience being the strongest. At last she finds an end at her fight of her mind when she marries Rochester.

GOOD (12 marks)

I agreed with the saying: "Today's luxuries are tomorrow's necessities," because of the truth it holds in its words, and I believe that till progress will exist they will never be out of fashion.

When the radio was first invented it was a luxury, but with the passing of time it has become so much part of our daily life, that it seems strange to think of someone never using it. The same thing stands for television, headphones, telephones, hairdryers and so on.

Many things that can be a novelty today, if useful, will soon be owned by everyone; and if someday we should miss them, the daily routine of our life is likely to be jeopardized. An example of this is if we should find ourselves in a place where there is no television and no radio. Soon, we would find ourselves expecting the Newspaper as if is were a treat, we would feel left out from international events and cut off from the rest of the world.

Everyday something new is created, something new invented, but our progress is so fast, that after no more than a year we are already looking with surprise at something else, already wandering what other surprises the future hold in store for us.

We are adjusting to progress so easily that for this reason whatever is a luxury today, may soon become a necessity tomorrow for all of us.

PASS (10 marks)

I always refuse to plan my holidays, because I am absolutely certain that something is going to happen. I remember two years ago, when some friends of mine asked me where I was going to spend my Summer holidays, and I said that I did not know, first of all because I had not enough money and then I had only two weeks time, so it had to be a place not very far from where I lived, there had to be nice people and also had to be not expeveve. "We have got the right place for you", they said. They started telling me their plans, I got so excited that I said all right I come with you.

I remember leaving the house very early in the morning, I had not many things with me, because we were going camping and I could take with me only the indispensable. I had never been camping before so I felt a bit worried but calm. We drove to the South, we are going towards the sun, we thought. After three hours driving we had a quick rest and then drove on. We were in the open country when a boy said, "can anybody smell burning?" after two miles the car suddenly stopped, there was no more water in the engine. We didn't know what to do because it was getting dark and there was nothing round us, just fields and fields. It was only next morning that we were able to contact somebody.

After the car being repaired, we searched for a nice spot to set out tend, at last we found it was the sea. We thought that we could not find a better place, there was as much sun and water as we wanted, and it was not very far from the village.

For two days everything went fine, the third day listening the weather forecast we heard of a storm approaching. We were not at all worried. It was about midday when it started raining, at first gust few drops but later on became worse and worse. Also the sea from smooth as it was became rough, and huge waves began to form. We started being afraid because we could hear the noise of the sea and gust of wind outside our tent. Somebody suggested to go out to see what was happening and every-body agreed. We had gust come out, running to find shelter somewhere, when we saw our tent completely covered by sea-water. A huge wave had swoop it away with everything that was inside it. We were lucky because we were safe but we had lost everything we had.

PASS (8 marks)

Some years ago some friends and I decided to do a long journey around Italy during our summer holiday. We had been organizing everything for a month and we were terribly anxious that all were well.

We wrote on a paper what we needed and we made a list of all places we had to visit day by day.

All seemed perfect and we enjoied thinking what a wonderful holiday it would have been.

At last such an expected day arrived. During the first day all was right till we arrived, tired but happy, in Naples in the evening. There began our troubles, first of all we couldn't find free rooms so that we were obliged to stay in our cars for all night. We were upset and a bit confused seeing a lack in our organization but the bad mood soon disappeared: the situation was only for that night!

The day after we visited some important places and all seemed well when suddenly someone snatched my bag. Of course nowadays these things happen very often in Italy, but you see . . . each of us had some responsability and in my bag there was all the money that needed for our food!

It goes without saying that I made a terrible fool of myself. I'm sure that in that moment some of my friends could kill me and not the thief. After a good half an hour full of a dangerous atmosphere, we decided to go back home earlier so that we could have enough money for our food.

This was the hope but the reality was another.

WEAK (7 marks)

My dear Sheila,

I am writing to you to you to express my dissatisfaction with the post I took up about a month ago. I don't know if you happened to read the advertisement that the Head master of the Modern Language Center advertised in the local newspaper of the 10th of May.

At the beginning I thought it would be marvellous to work in a school like this: I was offered lodging at the Centre, excellent conditions such as an air ticket and a high monthly salary: Well, as a result everything is right the opposite! Yesterday I had an argument with the boss as he rejected change: others teachers help to persuade him was useless!

Mouldy bread brought out a 15 year-old child in a terrible and unbearable rush! I made the kitchen closed down.

And moreover, what would you think of a Language school without a language laboratory when every singel student pays £500 a year to attend it!! One of these days the director will be flung into prison, I'll promise you! I am sure he is taking all that money for himself. I mean, he lives on his own and, nowadays, the cost of running a house is not so exorbitant! Believe me, Sheila, I am really on edge. During the night I don't dream anymore: I keep getting nightmares! I even went to see a doctor who prescribed me a mouth-treatment. "This should put you right" he told me and he advised me to take it easy.

But I can't live in this hell anymore.

Please, write to me as soon as you have time and sorry if I bothered you with my problems.

I am looking forward to hearing from you and I beg you to let me know if you hear of any other post.

With love,
Yours
Lucie

P.S. Is you mother still bed-ridden? Hasn't she recovered yet? Give her my best regards and much love.

VERY POOR (2 marks)

Dear
you remember how great was my delight when I have been offered the Job to teach at the Modern Language Center of Oxbridge. Now I am very disapointed in taking it. It is awful! it turned out to be another thing: the students are very upset and they claim that the conditions are not what they paid for. The boss of the center is rejecting charges. It is horible; very bad hygiene conditions and the kitchens are closed down. Another thing; stranded school staff is seeking redress and the Director absconds with funds. It is a shame!
  I do not know what do do in this situation. I would like you to advice me if I must leave the soonest possible.

Yours sincerely,

Exam preparation

Students should be given practice in writing compositions on all the different types of topics at the required length (200 to 350 words) and within the time available (about 1 hour). They should be trained to develop the skill of using language appropriate to different types of writing. This training should include exercises based on specific tasks. In the case of candidates intending to choose in the actual exam one of the topics based on optional reading, suitable practice questions should be devised for them to discuss and write about, based on the current syllabus (published in the Regulations each year). The questions in *Cambridge Proficiency Examination Practice 1* are based on 'sample books' and are simply included as illustrations and for practice by students who may have worked on these books in class.

Paper 3: Use of English (2 hours)

This paper has two sections: Section A contains exercises to test the candidate's active control of English usage and grammatical structure, while Section B consists of a number of questions testing comprehension and skill in summarising, based on a passage. The range of these exercises is illustrated in *Cambridge Proficiency Examination Practice 1*. (Up to 1983 there was also a directed writing exercise in this paper; this is now one of the topics from which candidates may choose in paper 2.)

Marking

Detailed marking schemes, based on a maximum mark of 80, with Section A carrying about 45 marks and Section B about 35, are given in the Teacher's Book of *Cambridge Proficiency Examination Practice 1*. Pass candidates may be expected to score 40 to 48 out of a 'raw' maximum of 80 (i.e. 20 to 24 marks out of the scaled total of 40).

Exam preparation

It should be noted that many of the exercises in Section A have more value as testing devices than as classroom exercises. Too much emphasis on such exercises in class may not increase students' language awareness or communicative skills. In particular, the modified cloze test (Question 1) should not be over-practised in class.

In preparing for Section B, students should be given practice in reading a wide range of texts from different sources and in answering questions on information given or implied and the language used. They should also practise summarising the information presented in texts, using their own words as far as possible and avoiding direct quotation.

Paper 4: Listening Comprehension (about 30 minutes)

The most radical change made in the examination syllabus for 1984 can be seen in this paper. Formerly an examiner read three specially written or adapted passages aloud to the candidates; now a cassette recording is played to them while they complete an answer sheet. Candidates listen to four or five authentic or simulated authentic texts, complete with all necessary spoken instructions; each text is normally heard twice on the cassette.

The texts include broadcasts, conversations, discussions, announcements and telephone calls, with speakers using both standard and non-standard speech styles. The questions include reordering or matching information, labelling and blank-filling, as well as multiple-choice and true/false questions. The questions test candidates' ability to extract information from the texts, to interpret the speakers' attitudes or intentions and to recognise the implications of stress and intonation patterns.

Marking

The final total of 20 marks gives, together with Paper 5, one third of the total marks in the examination. A complete marking scheme is given in the Teacher's Book for each of the practice tests.

Exam preparation

Students should become accustomed to the form and tempo of the recordings used in the examination. In particular, they should be exposed to recordings of speakers using unsimplified English, spoken at a natural speed. They should realise that understanding spoken English involves extracting the main points of information from a text and does not necessarily depend on understanding every word that is spoken. Classroom practice using task-based exercises is recommended.

Many of the recordings used in these practice tests and in the examination itself are taken from BBC World Service broadcasts. Wherever possible, students should be encouraged to listen to BBC World Service broadcasts in English. (Details can be obtained from the BBC, Bush House, London WC2B 4PH, or from any British Council office.)

The Teacher's Book contains transcripts of the recordings used in *Cambridge*

Proficiency Examination Practice 1. These are included only to help teachers to handle the tests confidently and see what each piece is about and how long it lasts. The transcripts should *not* be used to help students to 'spot the answers' to the questions. Many questions depend on interpreting what is heard on the tape, including the stress and intonation of the speakers which cannot be shown in a transcript.

Note: The recordings of the two cassettes that accompany *Cambridge Proficiency Examination Practice 1* follow the format of the exam exactly. Each text is heard twice with 15 seconds of silence before and after each hearing, during which students can read through the questions or task and write down their answers. There are also full spoken instructions on the cassettes.

Paper 5: Interview (about 15 minutes)

Paper 5 consists of three sections: in Section A the candidate converses about a photograph, in Section B a short prose passage is read aloud by the candidate and in Section C the candidate participates in a structured communication activity. The changes of syllabus in 1984 include increased weighting and time allowance for the Interview and change of format in the second two sections.

Provision is made for centres to opt for Section C of the Interview to be taken *either* in the usual candidate / examiner form *or* in groups of two or three candidates with an examiner. The added realism of a group Interview is strongly recommended although it is treated as an option. The increased amount of 'candidate talking time' generated and reduction in 'examiner talking time' mean that a group Interview involving three candidates can be accomplished relatively quickly and does not need to take longer than a single examiner / candidate interview. The examiner is thus also able to concentrate more on assessing the candidates and less on guiding (or leading) the conversation.

The same marking scales are used in assessing both FCE and CPE candidates in the Interview. The main difference is that CPE candidates are expected to demonstrate that they are capable of producing longer stretches of clear, coherent speech and of performing well in more complex or more serious discussions. The material that is used, particularly in Section C, is designed to give candidates the opportunity of demonstrating this ability.

Section A: Picture Conversation (about 5 minutes)

(This test is unchanged in 1984.) The examiner's version of the photograph has sets of suggested questions and follow-up topics. Not all of these need be used as long as candidates are given an opportunity to show their fluency. The conversation should move from specific commentary on the situation shown in the picture to associated themes, with the candidate encouraged to speak freely. Emphasis on the factual aspects of the photograph and questions about, for example, what is visible in the background should be avoided. It should be remembered that it is a candidate's language skills that are being tested, not his or her personality, intelligence or knowledge of the world.

In the Picture Conversation, a candidate's fluency and grammatical accuracy are assessed, following the scales shown below:

Fluency

5 4 —3— 2 1 0	Variation in speed and rhythm, choice of structures, general standard of expression completely (5) or mainly (4) effective and natural. At bare pass level and below, capable if unsteady or artificial (3), halting and unclear delivery (2), and complete incapacity for connected speech (1–0).

Grammatical accuracy

5 4 —3— 2 1 0	Control of a varied range of structures, including tenses, prepositions, etc., complete (5) or sufficient to sustain an effective level of expression (4). At (3) errors not basic, limiting rather than distorting expression. Below this errors predominate, impeding intelligibility (2), or showing no awareness of basic grammatical functions (1–0).

Section B: Reading Passage (about 3 minutes)

In this section candidates read a short passage aloud. They are given a few moments to look at the passage before being encouraged to identify its probable source and intention and then reading it aloud. The examiner assesses each candidate's pronunciation, stress and rhythm, following the scales shown below:

Pronunciation of individual sounds

5 4 —3— 2 1 0	Control of sound system* at near native-speaker level (5), coherent and consistent to an acceptable level (4), or with full intelligibility even if foreign (3). Incorrectness and foreign articulation impede understanding (2), or represent only a crude approximation to English sounds (1–0). *Proper differentiation of consonants (voiced and unvoiced) and vowels in stressed syllables; reduction of vowels in unstressed syllables; approximation to native-speaker timbre and basis of articulation.

Stress, rhythm and intonation

5 4 3 2 1 0	Stress timing and placing of stress, intonation patterns and range of pitch within sentence, natural linking of phrases at acceptable, near native-speaker level (5) or with clarity and control even though foreign (4). At (3) stress and intonation are unsteady; below this foreign speech patterns predominate with incorrect phrasing impeding (2) or preventing (1–0) intelligibility.

Section C: Structured Communication Activity (about 5 minutes)

This section consists of a range of communicative activities using a variety of visual and verbal stimuli. The range of activities, illustrated in *Cambridge Proficiency Examination Practice 1,* includes:

participation in a role-playing exercise based on a realistic situation;
exchanging information;
giving and exchanging opinions;
problem-solving discussions;
giving a short talk on a briefly prepared topic followed by a discussion;
talking about the optional reading.

It will be noticed that some of the activities in *Cambridge Proficiency Examination Practice 1* are based on fairly serious 'weighty' topics, such as politics or painting, while others are based on more straightforward 'mundane' topics, such as a murder mystery or hotels. Candidates at CPE level are expected to be able to discuss a wide variety of topics and to come closer to native-speaker competence than, for example, FCE candidates.

In these activities there is often an 'information gap' between the participants, leading to a realistic exchange of information and ideas between candidates (where the test is taken as a group), or between candidate and examiner. During the exercise candidates are given an impression mark on their vocabulary and communicative ability, according to the scales shown below:

Vocabulary

5 4 3 2 1 0	Resourceful and correct, in the context of the communicative needs tested (5), or mainly so (4). Vocabulary not sufficiently varied or at command, with hesitation and need to paraphrase (3), frequent inadequacy (2), or consistent breakdown over choice of words (1–0).

Communicative ability

5 4 3 2 1 0	(Marks in terms of general success with the given task, resourcefulness in meeting the unexpected, ability to elicit and communicate information in a competent manner and to function socially in a foreign language.) Flexibility and resource complete (5), sufficient (4) or adequate given special patience on the part of a listener (3). Communication too simplified or unreliable for real-life contexts (2) or quite inadequate (1–0).

Marking

In each section candidates are marked by impression on the aspects of their spoken English shown in the description of each section above. The 'raw' maximum of 30 is scaled to a final total of 40. An adequate mark may be thought of as about 60% of the total available (i.e. 18 out of 30).

Exam preparation

Students should be encouraged at all times in class to do more than just 'answer questions' and to participate actively in a variety of communicative activities and discussions. Working together in groups or in pairs is particularly valuable. Students may need special training in reading aloud short passages of the type used in Section B, though this should not be overdone.

In preparing for the Interview, students should be given experience of the whole interview as well as each of its sections. For Section C, group activities in class may be the most enjoyable way of doing this; but candidates who are taking the traditional candidate/examiner interview should be given experience of this too.

Note: The Student's Book of *Cambridge Proficiency Examination Practice 1* contains a selection of examination material (photographs, reading passages and communication activities) as presented to examination candidates, printed separately at the end of the book. This material is given in the Teacher's Book with each test, together with instructions for use. There are *two* items provided for each section of the test to give variety and extra practice.

Practice Test 1

Paper 1: Reading Comprehension (1 hour)

Section A   One mark for each correct answer

1 D	6 D	11 B	16 A	21 D
2 B	7 C	12 A	17 B	22 A
3 A	8 C	13 B	18 C	23 B
4 B	9 D	14 C	19 A	24 A
5 C	10 D	15 A	20 B	25 B

Section B   Two marks for each correct answer

26 C	32 C	36 B
27 C	33 B	37 C
28 C	34 A	38 C
29 D	35 B	39 D
30 A		40 B
31 D		

Total: 55

Paper 2: Composition (2 hours)

Give each composition a mark out of 20, according to the scale below. If necessary, look at the sample compositions on pages 5–9 for further guidance on the standards required at each grade in the marking scheme.

18–20	Excellent	Error-free, substantial and varied material, resourceful and controlled in language and expression.
16–17	Very Good	Good realisation of task, ambitious and natural in style.
12–15	Good	Sufficient assurance and freedom from basic error to maintain theme.
8–11	Pass	Clear realisation of task, reasonably correct and natural.
5–7	Weak	Near to pass level in general scope, but with either numerous errors or too elementary in style.
0–4	Very Poor	Basic errors, narrowness of vocabulary.

Total: 40

Paper 3: Use of English (2 hours)

A complete marking scheme is given for each question. Pass candidates would be expected to score at least 40 out of a maximum possible of 80. (The 'raw' total for the whole paper is adjusted to a mark out of 40 in the exam itself.)

Section A

Question 1

Deduct the total number of *incorrect* items from 10. Correct spelling is essential. Ten or more incorrect items score 0. No half marks.

1 ago/later/after	11 about
2 or/nor	12 the
3 led	13 to
4 only/really/single/most/one	14 For/Over
5 a	15 been
6 from	16 thought/conceived
7 more/also/purely	17 but/yet/if/though/although/sometimes
8 had *or* was	18 both
9 myself *or* everywhere	19 It
10 though/although	20 within/in/inside

Total: 10

Question 2

Give one mark for each word or phrase between the vertical lines. Ignore the words printed in italics.

a) *The inspector accused* | him | of stealing | *the jewels.*

b) *Unless* | it rains
it starts raining | *millions of pounds' worth of crops will be lost.*

c) *The bank robber threatened* | to shoot (the clerk)
that he would shoot the clerk | if he (the clerk)
moved. |

d) *According to* | the drama critic of the 'Daily News', | the new play is | *a major breakthrough.*

e) *Despite* | their good game
(their) playing well
the fact that they played well | *the team lost.*

f) *Galileo is regarded* | as (being) the father | *of modern astronomy.*

g) *Only by* | training hard every day | can you become
will you become
could you become | *a good athlete.*

h) *He is a* | more persuasive speaker/orator | *than his brother.*

Total: 12

Question 3

Give one mark for each correct word or phrase between the vertical lines, or two marks where shown. Ignore the words printed in italics.

a) *I've* | had one | *already.*
been given one
got one

b) *Seldom* | does the temperature fall | *below zero.*
has the temperature fallen
has the temperature dropped   (2 marks)
does the temperature go
has the temperature gone

c) *What* | has he been sent to prison | for | *?*
has he been arrested
has he been sacked/dismissed

d) *Difficult* | though/as it is | *it is not completely impossible.*
though/as it may seem to be
though/as it may appear to be
though/as it may be

e) *He took his car to the garage* | to have | *it repaired.*
to get

f) *You'd* | better go | *to the dentist's.*
best go

Total: 8

Question 4

Give one mark for each word or phrase between the vertical lines, or two marks as shown below. Ignore the words printed in italics.

a) |*I was (a) prey* | to | *obsessive and agonising thoughts.*
Obsessive and agonising thoughts | used to prey on me.
made me their prey.   (2 marks)

b) |*He is virtually* | illiterate.
blind.
unable to read.

c) |*His French is fluent enough* | *to go to the conference.*   (2 marks)
|*He is fluent enough in French*

d) *His arrival* | took us (completely) by surprise. |

e) |*The onset of the disease is* shown | *by a feeling of faintness.*
marked
indicated
characterised

f) |*At the outset, he gave* | *us a summary of his progress so far.*

17

g) |To offset their disappointment | *he bought them ice-cream.*

h) ||I travel by bus (only) as a last resort.
||I resort to travelling by bus (only) when I have no alternative. | (2 marks)

Total: 12

Section B

Question 5

Give the mark shown for each question for coherent and relevant answers.

a) He didn't know what he was eating. He didn't know elvers were baby eels.   2

b) It was unexpectedly appropriate to the miraculous story of eel reproduction.   2

c) People with theories about the origins of eels.   2

d) – The deliberate putting of horses' hairs in a stream.   2
   – That they bred from decaying matter.   2

e) Had their origin in.   1

f) Very free speculations with no possibility of proof.   2

g) Water flowing across the road. (eels = 0)   1

h) They were following each other in a long line.   1

i) It was the colour of the sea.   2

j) Willingly or not/they had no choice. (instinctively/inevitably = 1)   2

k) It was an inbuilt instinct as old as the species (1) and impossible to deny (1).   2

l) Their skins would burst (2) if they remained in shallow water/if they did not reach the sea (1).   3

m) It was dry and hard. (Non-specific answers e.g. 'difficult', and mention only of traffic dangers = 0.)   1

n) It was as accurate as human measurement could have made it.   2

o) One mark each for coherent inclusion of the following points, showing sense of correct order:
   – hatched in the ocean
   – swims 3,000 miles
   – grows up in river
   – changes colour
   – swims 3,000 miles to breeding area
   – mates, lays eggs and dies   6
   Give an impression mark out of 5 for expression and relevance.   5

Total: 38

Paper 4: Listening Comprehension (25 minutes)

First Part: Excursion announcement

		Score
2	9.15 / nine fifteen	½
3	12.00 / twelve o'clock, midday	½
4	6.00 / six o'clock	½
5	7.30 / seven thirty, half-past seven	½
6	11.00 / eleven o'clock	½
7	1.30 / one thirty, half-past one	½
8	C	1
9	D	1
10	C	1

Total: 6 marks

Second Part: A children's toy

		Score
11	D	1
12	D	1
13	A	1
14	C	1
15	B	1

Total: 5 marks

Third Part: Lost child

		Score
16	B	1
17	C	1
18	D	1
19	C	1

Total: 4 marks

Fourth Part: Sports report

Score

20 2 (Longchamps)   1

21

	Date	Race course	Country	
1	October 1st	Salisbury	England	
2	October 4th	Longchamps	France	1
3	October 12th	Kempton Park (annual team event part one)	England	1
4	October 24th	Belmont Park (annual team event part two)	United States/ USA/America	1

1 mark for each correct answer

Total: 4 marks

22

Carson	
Piggott	✓
Swinburne	✓
Starkey	✓
Mercer	✓
Eddery	✓

(One mark if all 5 jockeys are ticked. No marks if any missed.)

1

Total: 1 mark

Transcript

University of Cambridge Local Examinations Syndicate. This is the Certificate of Proficiency in English Listening Comprehension Test.

Test Number One

For the first part of the test you will hear an announcement. It's about a trip to Stratford. Look at questions 1–10. For questions 1–7 fill in the information in the spaces on the notepad. For questions 8–10 tick one of the boxes A, B, C or D. You will hear the piece twice.

pause

EXCURSION ANNOUNCEMENT

Excursion organiser: Could I have your attention for . . for a minute please? Thank you. Just two announcements this evening. Now on Wednesday, as you know, we have the excursion to Stratford-on-Avon, which I'm sure you've all been looking forward to. It's quite a long journey to Stratford, about three hours altogether, so it's very important that you should get away from here on time. I've asked the coach to be here at 9 o'clock, 9 a.m., and provided you're all on the coach and you can get away by 9.15, you should be in Stratford at 12 o'clock. All right? I've asked the hotel to supply you with packed lunches, so if you're feeling a little peckish you can eat on the way. Otherwise, there'll be plenty of time to eat when you get to Stratford.

Now, there are several properties in Stratford associated with Shakespeare and his family: his birthplace and Anne Hathaway's Cottage to mention just two. It would be difficult to see all of them in just half a day, so I'm afraid you'll have to make a selection. There's an admission charge at each of the properties, by the way. Dinner has been booked for 6 p.m. at the Bell Hotel. The . . the Bell Hotel. The cost of dinner is included, of course, in the fee for the excursion. The theatre is only a few minutes' walk from the Hotel, so you should have . . you should have no difficulty getting there in time for the performance, which begins at 7.30. Now, don't worry if you can't understand everything, most English people don't understand half of a Shakespeare play.

The coach will pick you up afterwards at about 11 p.m. and you should be back here at about 1.30. The traffic shouldn't be too heavy on the way back. Thursday morning will be a rest morning. All right?

Now the second item I wanted to mention was the disco dance next . . .

pause

Now you will hear the piece again. [The piece is repeated.]

pause

That is the end of the first part of the test.

Second Part
In the second part of the test you will hear a radio programme about children's toys. Look at questions 11–15. For each question tick one of the boxes A, B, C or D. You will hear the piece twice.

pause

A CHILDREN'S TOY

Tom: Well, this is my idea for a very cheap and . . um . . surprisingly very, very interesting and time-consuming toy. Children are not nearly as sophisticated in terms of exotic toys as . . um . . as people would have you believe. Now, this is just an ordinary piece of wood, and on it I've put a battery . . um . . a little, flat battery out of a torch. Um . . er . . 4½ volt, flat battery. A couple of cheap bulb holders, and . . um . . oh, one of the bulbs is painted green to make it a little bit different. A few odd bits of wires from the junk box . . er . . a few drawing pins . . um . . to act as terminals and . . um . . er . . by connecting the bits of wires that I've put between the bulbs . . er . . in different orders you can light one or both bulbs.

Bernard: Is that all you need?

Tom: Mm? Oh and an electric motor.

Bernard: Ah! How does it work, Tom?

Tom: Well, it's . . um . . it's, it's very, very simple. You, you connect wires together and bulbs light up, and this sort of thing, and er . . um . . it, it might seem not appealing to you, but you're over six years old, ahha . . and to the dad that likes to prove he can wire up things electric. Um . . er . . I . . I've also put on this, incidentally, it's a . . an electric motor out of a broken er . . um . . racing car, which connects to the battery . . er . . er . . like this . . and . . er . . whirrs round. I've stuck a little bit of paper across one of the axles of the . . er . . .

Bernard: Oh, very nice, Tom.

Tom: . . . electric motor and it flies round and . . er . . makes a nice noise. And also if . . er . . if you want to get complicated, you can . . um . . um . . demonstrate basic electronics or electrical engineering to yourself and then to your children, having . . um . . having learnt. I can make this bulb go bright and dim because I've wired the motor . . .

Bernard: So you can, yes!

Tom: . . . wired the motor in series with the bulb, so the battery drives both of them, and . . um . . if you get the engine whirring the bulb's . . um . . um . . slightly dim, but as you slow down the engine, the bulb gets brighter. Fascinating, er . . er . . don't . . don't you think, Bernard?

Bernard: Yes it's all happening there, isn't it?

Tom: Oh, certainly is! Haha. Ah.

Bernard: Well, I . . er . . I think I might . . um . . well, it's not too difficult to actually build. What . . um . . what kind of cost would you say?

Tom: Oh, well . . um . . er . . pence really. I . . I mean the sort of things that you might . . um . . might . . oh, the torch battery you could steal from . . um . . the . . the torch in the kitchen, maybe, but . . but, there's nothing . . .

pause

Now you will hear the piece again. [The piece is repeated.]

pause

That is the end of the second part of the test.

Third Part

In the third part of the test you will hear a woman telling an airport official about her lost child. Look at questions 16–19. For each question tick one of the boxes A, B, C or D. You will hear the piece twice.

pause

LOST CHILD

Woman: Oh . . oh, sir, can . . can you help me?

Man: Yes, madam, what's the trouble?

Woman: My . . my daughter's disappeared. She was just standing there and . . and I put my luggage down over there and then I came back and she'd gone and . . and she's not anywhere. I've been absolutely everywhere!

Man: I see.

Woman: And . . and I've called and called and she's just not there . . .

Man: All right, let's get a few facts, shall, we, madam?

Woman: And . . and . . I've been . . . I walked all up there and . . and gone there and she's . . . She's just gone . . .

Man: Your daughter, you say? Now what age is your daughter?

Woman: I . . I mean, she never usually wanders off like that. And I just don't know what happened.

Man: Yes, indeed, yes.

Woman: And . . and I'm really worried that somebody's just picked her up and . . and she's gone, you see! And I don't know what to do. All . . all I did was just put the luggage down, you know, and then I turned round and she'd gone!

Man: And where was this you say?

Woman: And there were a few people around. I . . I mean there was a funny man sort of wandering about and he disappeared and she disappeared and I . . I'm really worried . . .

Man: OK, madam. Right, now, where did this happen, madam? You say it was here?

Woman: . . .that he's taken her. It . . it was just over there. I . . . I put my luggage . . .

Man: Over there? You mean the check-in desk?

Woman: It was just over there. And I just put my luggage down and she disappeared.

Man: And it is your daughter?

Woman: She's my daughter.

Man: Right, now can we have some details?

Woman: She's my daughter!

Man: Yes, now can we have a few details? The sooner I get some details down, the sooner we'll find her. That's what we want, isn't it?

Woman: . . . I looked round and then she wasn't there. She's never walked away before!

Man: All right now, madam? Yes, now how old is your daughter?

Woman: I really don't understand what's happened.

Man: How *old* is she?

Woman: I don't know what my husband will say. Can I . . can I ring up my husband? Oh . . oh, no perhaps . . . Oh we ought . . we ought to find her first.

Man: Er . . yes, now . . as soon . . madam . . as soon as we get some details down madam, the sooner . . .

Woman: She's just gone! I just walked all over there and . . and I walked down there and she's just not there!

Man: Very good. Now, madam, can you tell me what's her name?

Woman: Katie.

Man: I see. And what's her age?

Woman: Four, four and a half – she . . she's nearly five.

Man: Yes, and what colour hair has she got? Your colour?

Woman: Well it . . it . . it's sort of brown.

Man: Your brown?

Woman: Yes, brown.

Man: Yes, brown. And . . er . . what's she wearing?

Woman: Do . . do you think we could go and look for her now, because you . . you see if we stand here answering questions . . you see she could have gone even further . . .

Man: Yes, madam . . . Madam! Madam, there are plenty of personnel in the airport, madam. The sooner we get her details down . . .

Woman: . . . she could be on a plane! Or . . or anything! I just don't know where she's gone . . .

Man: Please listen to me, madam. The sooner we get her details down, the sooner I can circulate them and there are hundreds of people, literally hundreds of people who will have them and she'll be found very shortly I promise you.

Woman: Yes . . all right.

Man: Now . . now where were we? Now, what was she wearing?

Woman: She . . she was wearing . . she was wearing her red dress with white dots on it.

Man: Yes, a red dress, white polka dots.

Woman: Her name's Katie.

Man: Katie, yes, I've got that down and she's 4½, brown hair.

Woman: She's 4½.

Man: OK, right. And you're booked out to where, madam?

Woman: I'm going to France!

Man: Your check-in . . . I see, you were at that check-in desk. Number 35. Right.

Woman: Yes. Yes.

Man: And that's where you missed her? I see, now, tell me: has she got a sweet tooth?

Woman: What!?

Man: I mean, she wouldn't have wandered off to the sweet shop or anything like that, would she?

Woman: No, no, no. She never wanders off like that. And that's why I'm so surprised!

Man: Right. Ah well, yes, well . . I've got kids of my own and we all say that until the first time they do. OK, now: Katie, brown hair, 4½, red dress, polka dots. Right, now you leave it with us, madam. Now don't worry, madam.

Woman: All right. Yes . . .

pause

Now you will hear the piece again. [The piece is repeated.]

pause

That is the end of the third part of the test.

Fourth Part
*For the fourth part of the test you will hear a sports item on the radio. Look at the racing
calendar and look carefully at questions 20–22. You will hear the piece twice.*

pause

SPORTS REPORT

. . . the end of the football results. Turning now to racing and the big news is what about
Starkey! He's been banned for one week as from today for careless riding at Salisbury and
this means he'll have to miss the big race in France which is scheduled for the 4th
October. It's the fourth time that Starkey has been suspended in thirteen months but the
ban will be over by the time the battle between British and American jockeys takes place
at Kempton Park. That annual event is due on the 12th October when five riders from
each team take part in a series of races. Willy Carson is injured and is replaced by Walter
Swinburne who joins Starkey, Lester Piggott, Pat Eddery and Joe Mercer in forming the
British team. The US will stage the second part of the series at Belmont Park.

pause

Now you will hear the piece again. [The piece is repeated.]

pause

That is the end of the test.

Paper 5: Interview (about 15 minutes)

For each section of this test paper a choice of exercises is given. This enables teachers to provide some variety for students using the tests and shows the range of different kinds of exercise that may be expected in the CPE exam itself.

Section A: Picture Conversation (about 5 minutes)

Ask candidates to look at one of the photographs shown below. They can both be found among the Interview Exercises at the back of the Student's Book: the first is number 1 on page 107 and the second is number 2 on page 108. Each candidate is assessed for **fluency** and **grammatical accuracy** according to the scales shown on page 12.

1

What is happening in this picture?
What kind of people are they?
Where do you think the photo was taken?
What do you think the woman is saying?
Why do you think the boys are listening so attentively?

The conversation should lead to to an informal discussion of one or more of the following subjects:

Cooking and food; education for boys and for girls; single-sex schools.

Questions like the following may help to lead the conversation in the right direction:

Have you ever had cookery lessons? What were they like?
What's your favourite dish and how is it prepared?
What kinds of food do you enjoy eating and why?
What school subjects should be taught only to boys, or only to girls?
What things are women better at doing than men and vice versa?
What do you think about schools where boys and girls are educated separately?

2

What is happening in this picture?
What are the people wearing and why?
Why do you think their hands and feet are unprotected?
If you saw them approaching you, how would you feel?

The conversation should lead on to an informal discussion of one or more of the following subjects:

Pollution; uniforms; clothes and fashion.

Questions like the following may help to lead the conversation in the right direction:

What kinds of pollution are problems in your city or town?
What can be done to combat the various kinds of pollution?
Which jobs require the wearing of special clothing or uniforms in your country?
Are uniforms necessary or are they just worn for traditional reasons?
How important is it for *you* to be fashionably dressed?
Describe your favourite outfit.

Section B: Reading Passage (about 3 minutes)

Ask candidates to look at one of the reading passages shown below. They can be found among the Interview Exercises at the back of the Student's Book. The first is number 11 on page 112 and the second is number 12 on page 112.

Before the passage is read aloud, candidates should be asked to consider, for example, what the subject of the passage is and who is speaking and why.

11 I'm not a reporter, but I am interested in talking to people when I'm visiting abroad and I'd like your views. You might call me an amateur politician, someone with an active concern over issues, especially health and safety issues. As it happens, we're a breed that my country produces in some quantity. But as you can guess, it makes life rather hectic when we start on each other.

12 I would attribute any success in my political career to the realisation that you learn more from your opponents than from your most fervent supporters. A politician's own associates will push him to disaster unless his enemies show him where the dangers are. If he is wise, he will often utter that old paradoxical prayer: God protect me from my friends.

Each candidate's **pronunciation** and **stress and rhythm** are assessed according to the scales shown on page 12.

Section C: Structured Communication Activity (about 5 minutes)

To show the range of activities that may be expected in this section, and to provide some variety for classroom use, there is a choice of three different exercises, each of which is suitable for use with groups of candidates *or* with candidates talking singly to the examiner. The third exercise in each practice test is a sample discussion based on the optional reading referred to in Paper 2 of each practice test. These exercises are designed for the following combinations of participants:

– 3 candidates and the examiner listening and prompting when necessary, as well as assessing;
– 2 candidates and the examiner participating as well as assessing;
– 1 candidate and the examiner participating and assessing.

All the exercises in *Cambridge Proficiency Examination Practice 1* give instructions for *group* interactions. If they are to be done as one-to-one interactions, then the teacher is expected to *participate* by using Student B's information and not simply asking questions as in Section A.

In chairing a discussion or prompting reticent candidates the examiner should avoid asking questions that can be answered with *Yes* or *No*. Prompts such as:

Could you tell us a bit more about that point?

Why do you think that?

Could you give us an example of what you mean?

I see, please go on . . .

will help to prolong each candidate's contribution and enable the examiner to assess their communicative ability and vocabulary range.

One or two minutes should be allowed for candidates to prepare each activity. If they wish, they may make notes to help them remember the points they want to make.

All the necessary information for participants in these exercises can be found among the Interview Exercises at the back of the Student's Book. Clear instructions on operating these exercises are given below.

First Communication Activity

Candidate A should look at Interview Exercise 21, candidate B should look at Interview Exercise 31 and candidate C should look at Interview Exercise 39. (If necessary or desirable, the group of three can include the examiner as the third member (candidate C) looking at the information in Interview Exercise 39 in the Student's Book.)

Each candidate in the exercise has a different paragraph from a newspaper article about the life and death of Arthur Hardwick, a newspaper tycoon who has died in mysterious circumstances. Allow them a minute or two to read their paragraphs and then ask them to explain their part of the story in their own words. Encourage them to ask each other questions and comment on each other's narrative in a friendly way. Then ask them to decide whether Arthur Hardwick's death was suicide, murder or an accident. Ask them to speculate who might have had a motive to murder him, and perhaps what punishment the murderer should receive. (The gun was under the note and someone who had shot himself in the head couldn't have put it there himself. However, someone who found the body could have put the gun there before the police came.)

During the conversation, each candidate's **vocabulary** and **communicative ability** are assessed according to the scales shown on page 13. As far as possible, the examiner should not intervene in the discussion unless candidates seem to be drying up or a reticent candidate needs encouragement.

Second Communication Activity

All candidates should look at Interview Exercise 22. Each candidate should be given a different part of the agenda to deal with. (In a one-to-one interaction the candidate may be asked to deal with several items on the agenda while the examiner, as a participant, deals with another item in the discussion.)

22 Imagine that you and the other members of your group are members of a committee that is responsible for the planning of a party which your class is organising for 30 children aged between 7 and 9 from a local school. The agenda below shows the details that need to be decided on at this committee meeting.

CHILDREN'S PARTY COMMITTEE MEETING

<u>Agenda</u>

1 Food and drink (buffet-style): what needs to be bought and how is the food to be prepared and when is it to be served?

2 Entertainment: what sort of music, games and dancing would be suitable?

3 Supervision: how will the children be transported to and from the party and how will they be supervised during the time they are there?

4 Time and place: where and when should the party take place and how long should it last?

The examiner will tell you which items on the agenda you are responsible for. Be prepared to make a statement of your suggestions before you have a discussion with the other committee members.

Allow a minute or two for candidates to prepare their contributions before asking them to play their parts in the meeting. The examiner may chair the meeting or allow the group to have a more informal discussion.

During the meeting, each candidate's **vocabulary** and **communicative ability** are assessed according to the scales shown on page 13.

Third Communication Activity (Optional reading)

This is a sample exercise to show the kind of thing that may be expected in the examination. Candidates in groups or alone should look at Interview Exercise 23.

23 'What could I have done?' Put yourself in the position of either King Claudius in *Hamlet* or Gabriel Oak in *Far From the Madding Crowd* and argue your case. Consider how a different course of action might have led to a happier outcome for you in the story.

Allow one to two minutes' preparation time and then ask each candidate to make a statement of his or her views before a general discussion develops. If there is insufficient material to sustain the discussion, ask candidates to consider how, for example, Queen Gertrude might have acted differently to change the outcome of the play. (This question can be adapted to refer to characters in other optional texts.)

Each candidate's **vocabulary** and **communicative ability** are assessed according to the scales shown on page 13.

Practice Test 2

Paper 1: Reading Comprehension (1 hour)

Section A One mark for each correct answer

1 C	6 A	11 C	16 D	21 B
2 A	7 D	12 B	17 C	22 A
3 B	8 D	13 B	18 B	23 C
4 A	9 D	14 A	19 A	24 B
5 D	10 A	15 A	20 A	25 B

Section B Two marks for each correct answer

26 C	32 D	36 B
27 A	33 C	37 C
28 D	34 C	38 C
29 C	35 C	39 D
30 B		40 A
31 B		

Total: 55

Paper 2: Composition (2 hours)

Give each composition a mark out of 20, according to the scale shown on page 4. If necessary, look at the sample compositions on pages 5–9 for further guidance on the standards required at each grade in the marking scheme.

Total: 40

Paper 3: Use of English (2 hours)

Section A

Question 1

Deduct the total number of *incorrect* items from 10. Correct spelling is essential. Ten or more incorrect items score 0. No half marks.

1 make	11 for
2 of	12 the/an
3 deal	13 to
4 all	14 off
5 to	15 as
6 in	16 with/of
7 by	17 of
8 same	18 in/by
9 that	19 as
10 people/those	20 a/some/one

Total: 10

Question 2

Give one mark for each word or phrase between the vertical lines, or two marks where shown. Ignore the words printed in italics.

a) *If I* | were you | *I would forget about buying a new house.*

b) *Eric told his girlfriend that* | he didn't love her any more. |
    | he no longer loved her. | (2 marks)

c) *He insisted* | on seeing | *the manager.*

d) *Arthur apologised* | for | hurting | *her feelings.*
    | | having hurt |

e) *It's* | time | I got | *back to work.*
    | high time | I went |
    | about time |

   |It's time for me to get/go back to work.| (2 marks)

f) *It* | hasn't rained for a fortnight. |
    | hasn't rained for two weeks. |
    | last rained a fortnight ago. |
    | last rained two weeks ago. | (2 marks)

g) *It was not* | until after midnight | that the noise next door stopped. |
    | till after midnight |

h) *The car was too* | rusty to repair. |
    | rusty to be repaired. |

i) *He's always* | short of money. |
    | hard up. |
    | broke. |

32

j)   *Yogurt is supposed to do* | you good. |

Total: 15

Question 3

Give one mark for each word or phrase between the vertical lines. Ignore the words printed in italics.

a)   *The children were* | looking forward | *to their holiday.*

b)   *His cold attitude showed that he was not* | used to | *being criticised.*
                                               accustomed to
                                               happy about
                                               overjoyed about |

c)   *I wish* | I had | *met him*   or   *I wish* | he | *etc.*
              I could have   she
              I had never   you
              I'd   we
              I'd never | they |

d)   *If only her father* | would | *agree I could marry her now.*
                          | were to |

e)   *I'll lend you the money as* | long as | *you promise to give it back.*

f)   *Don't* | bother to | *iron that shirt; it's a waste of time.*
             trouble to
             try to |

g)   *It might take him six months to* | get over | *his illness.*
                                       | recover from |

h)   *How long* | have you been writing/holding your racket/using a knife, *etc.* | *with your left*
                | have you written/held your racket/used a knife, *etc.* | *hand?*

i)   *You'll have to work hard to* | catch up | *with the rest of the class.*
                                   keep up
                                   keep pace |

j)   *I'd make you some tea but we seem to have* | run out | *of milk.*

Total: 10

Question 4

Give one mark for each word or phrase between the vertical lines. Ignore the words printed in italics.

a)   *Sarah wore dark glasses* | to avoid | being recognised.|
                                          | recognition. |

b)   *Anne was afraid the neighbours would* | look down on | *her for not having*
                                            | look down their noses at |
     a washing machine.

33

c) *If only you had* | made an effort | *you might have passed the*
made a greater effort | *exam.*
put more effort into your work, *etc.* |

d) | Would you mind opening | *the door for me?*
Do you mind opening |
I wonder if you'd mind opening |

e) *It might be better* | to leave out | *that paragraph.*

f) *Bill* | put his success down to | *incredible luck.*

g) *Why not tell him the truth and* | get it over with?
get it over and done with?
get if off your chest? |

h) | It was hard for Martin to accept | *the loss•of his money.*
Martin found it hard to accept |

i) | I didn't mean to | *upset you.*

j) *The children* | kept (on) asking (us) for | *sweets.*

Total: 11

Section B

Question 5

Give the mark shown for each question for coherent and relevant answers.

a) Having enough money isn't usually a problem.   1

b) a disastrous (1) preference/tendency, etc. (1) (NOT desire, wish, etc.)   2

c) The climate is extreme, therefore unhealthy. (idea of health essential, not just 'bones')   1
Houses have to be heated more, which is expensive.   1

d) Day-to-day, continual repairs/mending. (Allow examples; NOT upkeep of house and garden only.)   1

e) House actually begins to deteriorate.   1
'Crumble' usually used metaphorically/figuratively.   1

f) They are lonely and helpless.   1
To evoke sympathy.   1

g) They are likely to have relatives nearby to care for them.   1
Social services are better in big cities.   1
The climate is not ideal by sea.   1

h) To emphasise the point (1), which is often overlooked (1).   2

i) The house crawling with maggots/idea of squalor, etc. (1), which could be health hazard/offend social worker, etc. (1). (NOT just idea of personal freedom, etc.)   2

j) The older it is the more likely it is to go wrong/need attention/repair.   1
Even spare parts may be needed.   1

k) Make young (again). 1

l) Doctors are interested in technical problems, etc. (1), and disregard moral questions (1). 2

m) The problem/fact of old age/whether old age is happy or hellish. 1

n) Being happy depends on the individual's character (1), not on other factors (money or health, etc.) (1). 2

o) 1 mark each for inclusion of: – lack of resources (social services)
                               – values may be different (social workers)
                               – further explanation of *idea* of personal freedom
                               – decisions about what medical treatment is justifiable (doctors, scientists and society)
                               – decisions about how far to prolong life 5

    Bonus 1 each for: –conciseness
                          – high level of fluency
                          – avoidance of 'lifting'
                          – accurate spelling 4

Total: 34

Paper 4: Listening Comprehension (32 minutes)

First Part: Noise

		Score
1	C	1
2	A	1
3	D	1
4	D	1
5	A	1
6	C	1
7	B	1

Total: 7 marks

Second Part: Mayday

		Score
8	B	1
9	C	1
10	A	1
11	A	1
12	A	1

Total: 5 marks

Third Part: Tourist information

	You (sport)	Your friend (music)
13 Horseguards		
14 Crystal Palace National Sports Centre	✓	
15 St John's Wood	✓	
16 Cumberland Hotel		
17 Crystal Palace Football Ground		✓ *
18 Holland Park		✓
19 Hyde Park	✓	*
20 Round House		✓
21 Queen Elizabeth Hall		✓
22 Crystal Palace Concert Bowl		✓

½ mark for each correct row shown above

* Accept no ticks as correct also.

Total: 5 marks

Fourth part: Dangerous driving

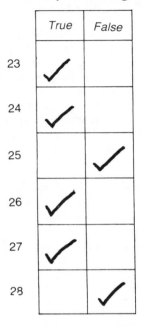

	True	False
23	✓	
24	✓	
25		✓
26	✓	
27	✓	
28		✓

½ mark for each correct row shown above

Total: 3 marks

Transcript

University of Cambridge Local Examinations Syndicate. This is the Certificate of Proficiency in English Listening Comprehension Test.

Test Number Two

For the first part of the test you will hear a radio programme about the problem of noise and what you can do in Britain if you are troubled by it. Look at questions 1–7. For each question you will have to tick one of the boxes A, B, C or D. You will hear the piece twice.

pause

NOISE

Presenter: The biggest environmental nuisance that most of us suffer from is almost certainly noise. According to government figures, six out of ten people in built-up areas say they suffer from unacceptable noise levels, and even in the heart of the countryside, you can't escape the distant hum of the motorway and the roar of the underpowered Japanese moped. In fact, traffic noise alone, say the latest studies, now affects over 11 million people. And in today's environment, as Susan Marling found out in one of London's leafier suburbs, you can be deafened by strange and several noises – all horrible.

Woman: At this time of year there's one in particular that drives me round the bend, and that is, when I'm sitting inside and, suddenly, there is a deafening

37

noise from the street, which comes from people with very loud car radios or multi-track stereos, or whatever they are, going flat out with all their windows wide open.

Interviewer: On a crowded little island like Britain it's not surprising that there are quarrels about noise. But, though noise is the new pollutant, you may be surprised to learn that in law you don't have the right to peace and quiet. Last Sunday afternoon, I spent a couple of deafening hours in my garden, the victim of DIY, yapping dogs, transistor radios, and the piercing accompaniment of a burglar alarm. (*noise*) Enough, you'll agree, to send the earthworms back into their holes, bugs into the woodwork, and me indoors. A quiet man who knows all about noise and nuisance is Richard McRorey, lecturer in environmental law at Imperial College. His advice to me was to keep a diary of the nasty noises if I wanted to get them stopped. But what do I do then, about that yapping dog, for example.

Mr McRorey: Your first step would be to ring up the local environmental health officer . . er . . in your district or London borough council. And tell him the position. With any luck, he may come round, and he may take some noise measurements, and he certainly has the power to serve enforcement notices on your neighbours, asking them to . . er . . try and keep the dogs quiet at certain times, and if it goes on and on, they can eventually be taken to court. Now, what may well happen is that the environmental health officer may say, 'Well, this is really a problem for you to sort out with your neighbour.' If this is the case, what I would first do is to try and come to a reasonable compromise with your neighbour. Um . . you must never get angry, or unreasonable, and certainly, what the law will never forgive you for doing is if you take retaliatory action; if you now start making a noise in the hope that will make things better.

Interviewer: Or barking!

Mr McRorey: Or barking yourself, maybe, or buying some enormous dog, er . . and trying to have your own back, that is where you'll get into a very serious position, and if you eventually went to court, you would not win your case.

Interviewer: Now the environmental health officer is obviously quite an important fellow. But how . . how do I get hold of him? I . . I've never seen an environmental health officer. I wouldn't know what one looked like.

Mr McRorey: Well, they . . they look fairly normal and they may be carrying a noise meter. It's true that they are extremely important officials in this area, who are employed by district councils or London borough councils, and you should be able to ring up the offices of your . . your local authority and say, 'Can I speak to the environmental health department, or the environmental health officer?' And indeed . . er . . many boroughs now have environmental health officers who are on duty all night, who will come round and deal with the complaint. And they have powers of . . .

Interviewer: So, if there's a party going on next door to my house, and I want it stopped now, you're suggesting I can ring up my local authority and get the environmental health officer out.

Mr McRorey: Theoretically, and he may well . . he may well come out, particularly . . er . . in the case of parties, if it's a party which is going on all night, unreasonable hours, or perhaps it's . . you've had a party every week at this same time going on, I would certainly complain to the environmental health officer, and, indeed, make sure some neighbours also complain. And he has the powers to come round, and, indeed, issue a notice immediately telling them to desist from the noise, or, at least, stop making such a noise, say, after midnight or some hours like that.

pause

Now you will hear the piece again. [The piece is repeated.]

pause

That is the end of the first part of the test.

Second Part

In the second part of the test you will hear a radio programme in which the origin of the radio distress call 'Mayday' is discussed. Look at questions 8–12. For each question you will have to tick one of the boxes, A, B, C or D. You will hear the piece twice.

pause

MAYDAY

Presenter: And now a letter from Mr Douglas Cage in London. He asks . . .
Reader: Can you explain the origin of 'Mayday'? I believe it comes from the French 'm'aider' ('help me'), but if this is the case, surely it should be 'aidez-moi'?
Presenter: Not necessarily, Mr Cage. Here's an extract from the proceedings of the International Radio Telegraph Convention of 1927: 'The radio telephone distress call, which consists of the spoken expression "Mayday", corresponding to the French pronunciation of the expression "m'aider" . . .' I'm told that this form, the imperative infinitive, meaning 'help me', is grammatically correct, though it could merely be a shortening of 'come and help me' ('venez m'aider').

The word was the brain-child of Frederic Stanley Mockford. Born in 1897, he served as a specialist in wireless telegraphy during the First World War. In 1919, the Air Ministry appointed Mr Mockford civilian wireless officer at Hounslow Aerodrome, the world's first civil airport.

In 1922, now at Croydon Airport, he was responsible for another 'first' – the talking-in and down of aircraft in bad weather. He was a pioneer in establishing international procedures and regulations for the use of wireless by aircraft, and with his staff devised quick means of direction-finding triangulation. Pilots could find their exact position by contacting Croydon, which obtained cross-bearings from Pulham and Lympne. Within 60 seconds, Croydon could relay the answer to the pilot; yet, as Mockford was to recall later, not everyone was pleased in the early days of commercial flying to be saddled with a radio on the plane. He said: 'To the pilot it was a new-fangled, unappreciated box of tricks, to the airline proprietor a waste of payload and maintenance cost. And although an early regulation made the carriage of the wireless compulsory, it did not say that it must be in working order. Almost anything could delay a departure except the Marconi engineer's plea for a moment to look over the gear'.

After a life devoted to the furtherance of radio communication, Mockford died in 1962. A largely unsung hero – his name doesn't appear in any of the standard reference works, he's buried in the village churchyard of Selmeston in East Sussex. The simple inscription on his tombstone reads: '1st March

1965. In memory of our beloved Frederic Stanley Mockford. 65 years. Air radio pioneer and originator of the distress call Mayday'.

pause

Now you will hear the piece again. [The piece is repeated.]

pause

That is the end of the second part of the test.

Third Part
In the third part of the test you will hear a recorded telephone announcement giving details of what there is to do on a particular day in London. Look at questions 13–22. For each question fill in the missing information. You will hear the piece twice.

pause

TOURIST INFORMATION

London is unrivalled when it comes to pageantry. There's a Guard Changing ceremony outside Buckingham Palace at 11.30 this morning or you could see the Mounted Guard Changing ceremony at Horseguards at 10 o'clock.

If you're keen on sport, there's plenty to choose from today. There's a complete programme of sport from athletics to volley-ball and equestrian events which are on at the Crystal Palace National Sports Centre with the London Youth Games which start at 10 o'clock this morning. If you enjoy watching cricket, in the John Player League, Middlesex is playing Kent at Lords Cricket Ground in St John's Wood. Play starts at 2 o'clock.

Are you interested in antiques? There's an Antique Fair today at the Cumberland Hotel, Marble Arch, where you might find what you've always been looking for.

If the weather is nice, why not go along to the Hampstead Open-Air Art Exhibition at Whitestone Pond on Hampstead Heath, where you'll find over 200 pictures and many crafts stalls? And if you're a keen record collector, why not drop into the Record Collectors' Fair today at the Crystal Palace Football Ground?

You're listening to 'What's On', a special guide to entertainment and events in London this Sunday, produced by the British Tourist Authority.

Do you fancy spending a relaxing afternoon listening to music in the open air? At Holland Park, at 2 o'clock this afternoon, there is a Steel Band Panorama. If you're more energetic, at 11 o'clock there's a guided walk around elegant Mayfair, which starts from the main entrance to Green Park Underground Station.

At 2 o'clock you can join a walk which will take you around Lambeth in order to explore Cockney London. Meet your guide at the main entrance to Westminster Underground Station.

In Hyde Park today horse-lovers will enjoy the Greater London Riding Horse Parade, a parade of riding horses and ponies to be judged for condition and turnout, which starts at 2 o'clock.

How about listening to some music this evening? Tonight's Henry Wood Promenade Concert takes place at the Round House with the London Sinfonietta playing music by Boulez, Ligeti and Kurtag. Otherwise, why not recapture the magic of Vienna tonight at the Queen Elizabeth Hall with the Johann Strauss Orchestra and dancers in costume?

There's music in the open air at the Crystal Palace Concert Bowl. The Philharmonia Orchestra presents a programme of music by Rossini, Grieg and Tchaikovsky, ending with the 1812 Overture, complete with special effects and fireworks.

You might prefer a guided walk this evening around the picturesque Hampstead Village and the Heath, which starts at 7.30 from the main entrance to Hampstead Underground Station.

You've been listening to 'What's On', a special guide to entertainment and events in London this Sunday, produced by the British Tourist Authority.

And for further information on activities of special interest to children in London, it's available on 246-8007. Thank you for calling.

pause

Now you will hear the piece again. [The piece is repeated.]

pause

That is the end of the third part of the test.

Fourth part

In the fourth part of the test you will hear a conversation between a policeman and Mr Peters. Look at questions 23–28. For each question you will have to tick whether the statements are true or false. You will hear the piece twice.

pause

DANGEROUS DRIVING

Mr Peters: Er . . in here, Constable. Do sit down.

Policeman: No, thank you, Mr Peters. As I said, sir, I've a few questions I'd like to ask you.

Mr Peters: Yes . . yes, of course, I'll . . .

Policeman: Er..you're the owner of the red car in your drive, I take it, sir?

Mr Peters: Yes, of course!

Policeman: Volkswagen Golf, Registration SM 369 4JL.

Mr Peters: Yes. But what's . . .?

Policeman: And . . er . . does anyone drive your car besides yourself, sir? Your wife, perhaps?

Mr Peters: Oh, no, no one. I . . I'm not married.

Policeman: I see. So could you confirm, Mr Peters, whether or not you were driving your car last Monday afternoon on the B127 road . . er . . going towards Westwater from the direction of Minton?

Mr Peters: Last Monday? Um . . what date was that, now?

Policeman: Er . . the 7th April, Sir.

Mr Peters: The 7th . . um . . what was I . .? Oh, the dentist! Yes, yes, that's right! I did go to Westwater – I had a dentist appointment there at quarter to five.

Policeman: Mmm. So you started out at . . er . . er . . what time of day?

Mr Peters: Um . . I . . I'm not sure – about . . um . . half-past four from here, I suppose.

Policeman: Mm. You . . you didn't leave yourself much time for a 15-mile journey, Mr Peters. What time did you reach Westwater?

Mr Peters: Well, I . . I was a bit late. I . . I got there at about . . um . . about ten to, I'd say.

Policeman: Ten minutes to five at Westwater, you think, Sir. Well, I . . I'm trying to establish the approximate time you were driving along the half-mile stretch between Whitebridge and the new roundabout.

41

Mr Peters: Oh, I see. Um . . well, I wouldn't know exactly . . er . . let me see . . er . . that's about six miles out of Westwater, isn't it? Um . . it must've been nearly quarter to five, then, but . . .

Policeman: 4.45 approximately, yes, sir.

Mr Peters: Look, constable, suppose you tell me what all this is about?

Policeman: Well, the point is, Mr . . er . . Peters, I'm following up a report of alleged dangerous driving on the B127 to Westwater, between Whitebridge and the roundabout, on Monday 7th April at . . er . . 4.40 p.m. or thereabouts.

Mr Peters: Oh! Oh, I see.

Policeman: I don't need to remind you, sir, that's a particularly dangerous bit of road. There is a reduced speed limit, and no overtaking both ways.

Mr Peters: Yes, yes, I'm, aware of that. But I . . I'm sure I . . .

Policeman: What I'd like to know, Mr Peters, is whether *you* noticed any, what you might call, dangerous driving in the vicinity, at that time?

Mr Peters: Oh! Oh, you mean – did I witness anything you mean?

Policeman: Yes.

Mr Peters: Oh, well, um . . let me think now . . .

pause

Now you will hear the piece again. [The piece is repeated.]

pause

That is the end of the test.

Paper 5: Interview (about 15 minutes)

Section A: Picture Conversation (about 5 minutes)

Ask candidates to look at one of the photographs shown below. The first is number 3 and the second is number 4 among the Interview Exercises at the back of the Student's Book. Each candidate is assessed for **fluency** and **grammatical accuracy** according to the scale shown on page 12.

3

What's happening in this picture?
What kind of people can you see in the picture?
Why is this happening?
What do you think is going to happen afterwards?
Has anything like this ever happened to you?

The conversation should lead on to an informal discussion of one or more of the following subjects:

Practical jokes; humour; swimming and other water sports.

Questions like the following may help to lead the conversation in the right direction:

How would you feel if you were about to be thrown into a river?
Do you disapprove of practical jokes like this? If so, why?
What sort of things make you laugh?
How important is it to be able to swim and why?
What kinds of water sports do you enjoy and why?

4

What's happening in this picture?
What kind of people are they?
What do the things on the table tell you about the people and the situation?
What do you think they are talking about?

The conversation should lead on to an informal discussion of one or more of the following subjects:

Conversation; leisure; homes.

Questions like the following may help to lead the conversation in the right direction:

What kinds of things do you enjoy discussing with friends?
How do you spend your free time?
What's your idea of a 'perfect evening'?
Describe the living room in your own flat or house.
What makes a room feel welcoming and comfortable?

Section B: Reading passage (about 3 minutes)

Ask candidates to look at reading passage 13 or 14 among the Interview Exercises at the back of the Student's Book.

Before candidates read one of the passages aloud, they should be asked to consider, for example, what the subject of the passage is and who it was written or spoken by.

13   The brain does so much at a subconscious level. For example, the eye changes its curvature to focus on distant objects or near ones, and it's not merely the lens but the pupil around that is self-adjusting. The miracle is that this delicate process goes on all the time and yet we are utterly unconscious of it. We in no way have to will it to happen.

14   I don't think you can blame the cat. All cats need exercise to sharpen their claws, and a cat kept in a city flat needs a special scratching post. Get one made, train your cat to use it (cats can be trained to understand commands), and it will expend its energies on the post and not on the furniture.

Each candidate's **pronunciation** and **stress and rhythm** are assessed according to the scales shown on page 12.

Section C: Structured Communication Activity (about 5 minutes)

In this section, each candidate's **vocabulary** and **communicative ability** are assessed according to the scales on page 13.

First Communication Activity

Candidate A should look at Interview Exercise 24, candidate B should look at Interview Exercise 32 and candidate C should look at Interview Exercise 40. (If there is no candidate C, candidates A and B may also look at the information in Interview Exercise 40.)

Each participant in this activity has some information about an African country. The examiner is asked to play the role of someone who is thinking of applying for a job in one of the countries described and should ask the candidates for advice on the living conditions there. Much of this advice will be based on speculation and common sense as well as on the information given.

Second Communication Activity

All candidates should look at Interview Exercise 28.

28   Look at these three opinions of politicians:
'Politicians are the same all over. They promise to build a bridge even where there's no river.' (Nikita Khrushchev)
'I have come to the conclusion that politics are too serious a matter to be left to the politicians.' (Charles de Gaulle)
'The more you read about politics, you've got to admit that each party is worse than the other.' (Will Rogers)

Everybody seems to blame the politicians for what goes wrong in the world. What do *you* think of them?
Would you like to be one? Give your reasons why or why not.
What are the qualities of a good politician?
Which politicians, past or present, do you admire most?

Prepare a short talk (no longer than a minute) to introduce your ideas. If you like, you can concentrate on just one of the questions asked above.

Allow candidates a minute or two to prepare their ideas and make any notes they wish. Then chair the discussion, encouraging each candidate to speak at some length on the particular issues raised which interest him or her most. As far as possible, do not guide the discussion too much, except when one candidate seems to be dominating the others and you want to bring the more reticent candidates into the discussion.

Third Communication Activity (Optional reading)

For this sample activity, candidates should look at Interview Exercise 29.

29   'Literature is more concerned with relationships between people than with stories or ideas.' To what extent do you agree with this view? How can it be applied to the text you have read? Give examples to support your views.

Allow one or two minutes preparation time before asking each candidate to make a statement of his or her views. Allow candidates to comment on each other's contributions in a friendly way and to discuss the subject with as little interference from the examiner as possible. If there is insufficient material to sustain the discussion, ask candidates to comment on the view that 'Literature is the art of writing something that will be read twice'.

Practice Test 3

Paper 1: Reading Comprehension (1 hour)

Section A   One mark for each correct answer

1 C	6 C	11 D	16 C	21 A
2 D	7 C	12 A	17 B	22 B
3 D	8 B	13 A	18 A	23 C
4 B	9 C	14 A	19 D	24 C
5 A	10 B	15 B	20 B	25 A

Section B   Two marks for each correct answer

26 B	32 D	36 D
27 B	33 B	37 C
28 C	34 C	38 A
29 A	35 B	39 C
30 D		40 D
31 B		

Total: 55

Paper 2: Composition (2 hours)

Give each composition a mark out of 20, according to the scale shown on page 4. If necessary, look at the sample compositions on pages 5–9 for further guidance on the standards required at each grade in the marking scheme.

Total: 40

Paper 3: Use of English (2 hours)

Section A

Question 1

Deduct the total number of *incorrect* items from 10. Correct spelling is essential.

1	more	11	mirror
2	the	12	in
3	In	13	if/whether
4	their	14	without
5	set	15	should/must
6	under	16	them
7	this	17	especially/particularly
8	called/termed/considered	18	something/the
9	although/though/while/however	19	to
10	of	20	make

Total: 10

Question 2

Give one mark for each word or phrase between the vertical lines. Ignore the words printed in italics.

a) *Despite* | the play's good notices, | *not many people went to*
the fact that the play received good notices, | *see it.*
the good notices the play received,
| Despite (the) good notices, not many people went to see the play. |

b) *My father speaks hardly* | any English. |

c) *He denied* | stealing | *the car.*
having stolen
that he had stolen

d) *Now I wish (that)* | I hadn't asked | *her to stay.*
I had not asked

e) *The source* | of the information | could not be traced. |
couldn't be traced. |

f) *Whenever* | he comes to visit us | there's trouble. |
there is trouble. |

g) *Isn't there* | another way | to | *the city centre?*
some other way | to reach
any other way | of reaching
a different way
an alternative way

h) *At no time* | did he suspect (that) | the money had been stolen. |
someone had stolen the money. |

48

i) *Never in* | my life | have I seen | *such a mess!*
           all my life
           my whole life
           my entire life

j) *Does your aunt* | really need | to be met | *at the station?*
                    really want | us to meet her
                               someone to meet her
                               you to meet her
                               me to meet her
      Does your aunt | have to be met at the station? | (2 marks)

Total: 15

Question 3

Give one mark for each word or phrase between the vertical lines. Ignore the words printed in italics.

a) *You'd* | better | *go to bed for a while.*

b) *You* | have known him | *for a very long time, then.*
        've known him
        have known each other
        've known each other

c) *This bottle is nearly empty: you* | must have drunk | *a lot!*
                              seem to have drunk
                              have obviously drunk

d) *He's not* | used to going | *to bed so late.*
              accustomed to going
              in the habit of going

e) *He was given a high honour* | in recognition of | *his services to the country.*

f) *The trouble is that* | whatever | *he says, his wife disagrees with him.*
                  no matter what

g) *The instructions said that you* | should | take | *two pills every four hours.*
                                 could
                                 were to
                                 had to
                                 were supposed to

                                 shouldn't | take more than | *two pills every*
                                 weren't to | | *four hours.*
                                 weren't supposed to

h) *'I must be going.* | How about | *you?' 'No, I think* | I'll stay | *a bit longer.'*
                      What about | | I'll hang on

Total: 10

Question 4

Give one mark for each word or phrase between the vertical lines. Ignore the words printed in italics.

a) | It doesn't matter to them which film they go to. |
   | Which film they go to doesn't matter to them. |

b) | He went on talking | *even though no one was listening.*
   | He went on telling his story |
   | He went on with his story |

c) | If you/people didn't keep interrupting | *I'd finish the job quickly.*
   | If you/people stopped interrupting |

d) *The notice said that* | smoking in class was forbidden. |
   | it was forbidden to smoke in class. |
   | we were forbidden to smoke in class. |

e) *My mother* | disapproved of | *my new shoes.*

f) | She lost the job | *because her typing was poor.*
   | She lost her job |

g) | The thing which impressed me was the confident way he spoke. |
   | He spoke confidently, which impressed me. |
   | The confident way in which he spoke impressed me. |

h) | She can't tell | margarine from butter. |
   | the difference between margarine and butter. |

i) | He is an authority | on primitive religion. |

j) | He didn't contribute (anything) to the discussion. |

Total: 12

Section B

Question 5

Give the marks shown for each question for coherent and relevant answers.

a) Having one's skin turned brown (paraphrase of 'tanned' essential) (1)
   by the sun/while sunbathing (1).   2

b) Sunshades (essential) (1) are not available/cannot be bought (1).   2

c) Cosmetics   1
   Clothing   1
   Medical/pharmaceutical/makers of spectacles, lamps, pills, etc.   1
   Tourism, etc.   1

d) She was alive/famous before the 1920s.   1
   She was a member of high society/fashionable.   1
   She was pale, etc.   1

e) The idea of worship of sun, religion, etc.   1

f) The commercial exploitation of sunshine, etc. (paraphrase of 'trade' essential)   1

g) So crowded people lie almost touching.   1
So many cars they almost touch.   1

h) The French Riviera/Côte d'Azur. (no additions)   1

i) Pleasant climate/escape from winter   1
Casinos   1
For social reasons (allow lifting)   1

j) Ordinary people, people without money (no lifting)   1

k) The people who still frequented the Riviera after others had left. (essential)   1
Aristocrats, etc.   1

l) One mark for the inclusion of the following points:
   – sun became fashionable
   – more visitors than in winter/summer more attractive than winter/effect on hotel
     seasons
   – informality of clothes
   – tourist parties/visitors low class, not aristocrats
   – no longer luxury prices
   – retired prole went to live there/more interest in buying and renting property
   – development of camping   7
   plus 4 marks for impression – reward attempts to paraphrase, and
   concise expression.   4

Total: 33

Paper 4: Listening Comprehension (31 minutes)

First Part: Missing luggage

    Score
1 B   1
2 C   1
3 D   1

Total: 3 marks

Second Part: Drivers' championship

    Score
4 3,1,2   1
5 Accident – or words to that effect   1
6 Watson   1
7 Rosberg   1

Total: 4 marks

Third Part: Gardening advice

8 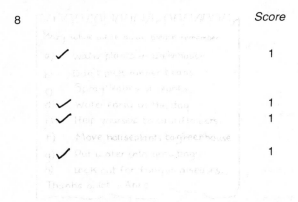   *Score*

                                                                1

                                                                1
                                                                1

                                                                1

Deduct a mark for each instruction incorrectly ticked.

9 C   1

Total: 5 marks

Fourth Part: Old people

     Score
10 C   1
11 A   1
12 A   1

Total: 3 marks

Fifth Part: Kiri Te Kanawa

     Score
13 B   1
14 C   1
15 D   1
16 C   1
17 B   1

Total: 5 marks

Transcript

University of Cambridge Local Examination Syndicate. This is the Certificate of Proficiency in English Listening Comprehension Test.
Test Number Three
For the first part of the test you will hear two people talking in an airport. Look at questions 1–3. For each of the questions you will have to tick one of the boxes A, B, C or D. You will hear the piece twice.

pause

MISSING LUGGAGE

Announcer:	Passengers from British Airways flight 54 from Johannesburg may now collect their luggage from carousel number 2 . . .
Woman:	Hello, I . . I wonder if you could help me. I've just come in from Montevideo, from Uruguay.
Man:	Well, I'm sorry, madam, I've just finished my shift and I'm just going for a cup of tea.
Woman:	Oh . . er . . well could you just wait a moment because I . . I've just . . .
Man:	Make it quick.
Woman:	Er . . yes, OK. It was just that I couldn't see anybody else around here, and I came in from the flight from Uruguay about 45 minutes ago, and I've been waiting for my luggage and it hasn't come through. Er . . do . . do you think you could phone through or see if there's any more luggage to come?
Man:	Well it's not really anything to do with me, I mean you've just got to wait there till it comes through.
Woman:	No, look I realise that, it's just that I can't see anybody else in the airport, and everyone else from my flight has picked up their luggage and they're now going through customs, but mine hasn't come and it's absolutely vital I get it because I'm going to a very important conference tomorrow. Well, anyway, I know it was loaded on in Uruguay . . .
Man:	Well, how long have you been down there?
Woman:	Well, the flight got in about 50 minutes ago and I've been standing at the luggage conveyor belt for 45 minutes.
Man:	Well . . er . . .
Woman:	And everybody else has picked up theirs and mine hasn't come and I know that it went on and we only stopped in Rio and then straight on to London.
Man:	Well, really there's not much I . . .
Woman:	And I wondered if you could phone through and see if it's been delayed or what's happened.
Man:	Well, it's not really my job to phone through, it's not my responsibility.
Woman:	Look . . look, I realise that but you must realise I've got to do something . . .
Man:	Look, I'm sorry, you'll just have to go and wait. I want to go for a cup of tea.
Woman:	Well, look, I'm sorry, but what am I supposed to do? I've been waiting there and of course I realise that there are delays, it may have been packed on last and so it's going to be last off the plane, you're the only official I can see sitting round here. There's absolutely no one else to help me. What am I supposed to do? My luggage hasn't arrived! Now look this is very important, would you please telephone or find out what has happened to my luggage, I've got to have it.

Man:	Well, it's no good shouting at me, because I don't know what's happened to your luggage.
Woman:	Look, I'm sorry, I'm not shouting at *you*, but surely you're representing the airline, I've paid a lot of money.
Man:	I know that.
Woman:	I have two pieces of luggage with very important papers. I've got to have it.
Man:	Well, really, I don't know what to suggest I . . I mean, I suppose . . .
Woman:	Well, look, I certainly don't. I mean, am I supposed to go and check the plane or look on the tarmac or something? What . . what can I do? I must have my luggage, everyone else has left and gone through customs!
Man:	Well . . well, all right I'll tell you what I'll do: if you go and sit down on that chair I'll see if I can get the manager, and tell him the problem.
Woman:	Yes, well, would you please immediately because I'm being met at the airport and I don't know what my friends will think.
Man:	Yeah, all right, all right.
Woman:	I'm late as it is.
Man:	Don't . . don't get angry. I'll go and get the manager now.
Woman:	No, well, I'm sorry it . . it's just that everyone else has gone through, and there doesn't seem to be anyone helpful round here.
Man:	All right, all right, I'll go and get the manager, that's fine.
Woman:	Well . . .
Man:	If you go and sit down quietly, and calm yourself down.
Woman:	OK. Thank you. Right, if you'd do it immediately I . . I'd appreciate it, thank you.
Man:	Right, fine, lovely . . .

pause

Now you will hear the piece again. [The piece is repeated.]

pause

That is the end of the first part of the test.

Second Part
For the second part of the test you will hear an extract from a radio sports programme. Look at questions 4–7. Answer the questions in the spaces provided. You will hear the piece twice.

pause

DRIVERS' CHAMPIONSHIP

Presenter:	Next Saturday evening sees the final round of the world motor racing championships, and once again the drivers' championship has remained open until the end of the season, because Watson still has a chance of beating Rosberg. The championship may be decided, though, not on a track, but in a French civil court. Richard Simons explains.
Reporter:	Rosberg leads the world championship table. Didier Pironi is second, three points behind, but he's been out of racing ever since that horrifying Hockenheim accident in August, and in third place is Watson, nine points behind Rosberg. Now for him to be champion, Watson will have to win on Saturday and Rosberg will have to score no points. They will then tie and Watson will then be declared the winner on the basis of more outright wins.

But it isn't as easy as that. Rosberg finished second in the Brazilian Grand Prix, way back near the beginning of the season and earned six points, but then he and the winner Nelson Piquet were later disqualified for having topped up their controversial brake cooling water tanks after the race. Without the additional water their cars might have been under weight at the post-race scrutineering. This practice had been an accepted ploy for some time, but a protest from Renault brought it all to a head. Rosberg's team boss, Williams, appealed against the disqualification, lost the appeal and sued the organising body in the French courts. If the decision goes Williams' way, Rosberg will be unbeatable and the drivers will arrive to learn that the new champion has already been crowned.

pause

Now you will hear the piece again. [The piece is repeated.]

pause

That is the end of the second part of the test.

Third Part

For the third part of the test you will hear a telephone information report about gardening. Look at questions 8 and 9. For question 8 tick the correct instructions according to the gardening expert. For question 9 tick one of the boxes A, B, C or D. You will hear the piece twice.

pause

GARDENING ADVICE

Hello, this is your gardening adviser.

Now, just as our gardens are at their most colourful, and most productive, what do we do? We go off on holiday and we leave them to their own devices. And in order to avoid a catastrophic loss of crops, and possibly plants as well, it is advisable to plan ahead. So, let's take the outdoor garden first. Crops such as runner beans, peas, marrows and cauliflowers and so on, that are coming ready, they'll not wait until you return from holiday, and unless they are eaten they will run to seed, and in the case of runner beans for instance, the plants will cease flowering prematurely.

Now, what I suggest you do is this, invite a friend or neighbour to help himself to your produce. You'll be doing both yourself and him a favour. Then in exchange for the goodies, you can ask him to water the plants in the greenhouse and in the frame until you return, but make sure first that he knows how to do it. That he should put water into the pots or into the rings, or into the growbags, or whatever the plants are growing in. What he should not do is throw water about indiscriminately over the leaves of the plants themselves, because if he does that tends to invite fungus diseases.

And also for the same reason, ask him if he possibly can, to water in the morning, rather than in the evening. Now that leaves houseplants. If you have a greenhouse or frame they can be transferred to either, and your same friendly neighbour can be asked to water them. But if you haven't got a greenhouse or a frame, there is one safe and easy way to keep the plants ticking over in your absence, and this is how you do it.

Place a six inch deep layer of newspaper in the bottom of the bath. Yes, the bath! Turn the tap on and keep the water flowing until the papers are absolutely sodden, thoroughly

soaked, now put the pot plants to stand on the wet paper, go off on holiday and they should be alive and well when you return in two weeks' time.
Thank you for calling. Till the next time, goodbye and good gardening!

pause

Now you will hear the piece again. [The piece is repeated.]

pause

That is the end of the third part of the test.

Fourth Part
For the fourth part of the test you will hear part of a radio programme about the problems of ageing. Look at questions 10–12. For questions 10–12 you will have to tick one of the boxes A, B, C or D. You will hear the piece twice.

pause

OLD PEOPLE

Presenter: For many years to come it will be the age of the aged. More and more people are getting older and older, and today one organisation publishes a document called 'Getting Old', which draws attention to the problem of an increasingly elderly population and the decreasing resources to cope with them. With me is the author of the document, Anne Good. Anne, if you could give us an idea first of the problem and the size of the elderly population that we have now.

Anne Good: Well, it's an enormous problem because it's come upon us so very rapidly. In . . um . . 1951, for instance, there were less than 7 million old people in this country, but by 1971 that had gone up to a horrendous 9 million, and it's still rising. It . . it isn't just old people because we think of everybody – foolishly I think – over 65 as being elderly, but it's the very old, those who are over 85, they're going to go up by 66%.

Presenter: And the point that you make in your document is that there's been an apparent lack of planning to cater for these, which should surely have been foreseen.

Anne Good: Oh, yes, we . . we find this quite appalling in our org . . organisation because these figures come as no surprise; I mean, we've known for a very long time that we were going to have what is an old age explosion. I mean, I remember in 1974 seeing figures which were put out by the DHSS showing alarming statistics but nothing's been done to plan for it.

Presenter: Now where is the greatest need – is it a medical need or a welfare need or what?

Anne Good: Well, it's a mixture, you see, because when you get old it . . it's very difficult to separate medical from welfare because the doctors rely on the home helps or else their patients have to go into hospital, but we feel that the planning must start at the GP level, because it's the general practitioner who can keep his elderly patients at home and happy. If that patient has to go into hospital, well, the costs are just horrendous.

pause

Now you will hear the piece again. [The piece is repeated.]

pause

That is the end of the fourth part of the test.

Fifth Part
For the fifth part of the test you will hear a music critic talking about the opera singer, Kiri Te Kanawa. Look at questions 13–17. For questions 13–17 tick one of the boxes A, B, C or D. You will hear the piece twice.

pause

KIRI TE KANAWA

David Fingleton: She was very successful indeed as a popular singer, there was no need for her from the immediate . . er . . financial economic point of view to go on to England to train to be an opera singer. She was being awarded golden discs and . . er . . filling any night club or open air stadium she cared to appear at and any town hall she cared to appear at, she was one of the best known young women in New Zealand.

Presenter: So your story, though it is obviously a success story is also the story of a struggle to be a suc . . that sort of success, a real struggle.

David Fingleton: Oh yes, because I think it was very hard for her in the . . and one reads the book one sees that . . um . . the early days in London were probably the hardest days she's ever had in her life because . . um . . she got to London as a very successful local celebrity in New Zealand and a girl capable of earning quite a lot of money, never having had a formal education to speak of, never having done a formal musical training, just her singing lessons with Sister Mary Leo. Suddenly being plunged into the London Opera Centre where most of the other students of course were graduates of either the universities or the music colleges and working damned hard towards careers which they hoped to get, never having earned anything in their lives up till then. And they regarded Kiri as rather spoilt and rather too well-off and a girl who could leap back to New Zealand and cut another long-playing record to . . um . . buy a few more frocks and . . um . . Kiri herself was somebody who wasn't used to a . . a . . student's curriculum and wasn't really prepared, in the first stages, to work at it.

Presenter: You say . . quite a lot about, I mean, nobody can help saying, what marvellous looks she had to go with her marvellous talents. Sometimes this obviously hasn't been entirely helpful. I mean, you..for example in some . . you say she looks so like a princess that singing Mimi, a sort of tubercular seamstress, is . . .

David Fingleton: Yes, I think Mimi is a difficult one for her to put across, not so much because of looking like a princess as because she's one of the healthiest people one knows and . . um . . she's very, very hard pushed not to look healthy.

Presenter: You say that her great resources are her confidence in her voice which is absolute, you say, and also her response to an audience.

David Fingleton: Yes, I think of all singers that I know she is the one who really empathises with an audience and can go out to them, they mean something to her; I think for that reason although she does her recordings jolly well she finds recordings harder work. She loves an audience. I remember when she was singing back in 1980 in the new production of Simone Boccanegra at Covent Garden and Mirella Freni suddenly had to go back to Italy in the middle of her run of La Bohème and they said to Kiri, 'Would you take over just to help us out one night as Mimi?' which of course was in no way contemplated or prepared and she said, 'Provided you give me the right prompter, the one I know, I'll do it'. And I was there, and it was one of the best performances of Mimi I've ever seen her give because she was facing the challenge of the audience and it was coming across.

Presenter: It must be said, er . . everybody says how dangerous it is to embark upon the biography of a living person. Did you find it dangerous?

David Fingleton: Well, yes, the . . the biggest danger was the person was so very much alive and a highly . . um . . critical and inquisitive audience and the first . . um . . section of my draft that I sent down to Kiri was with considerable fear and trepidation but . . um . . I was rung up the next morning at ten past eight saying, 'It was marvellous, I couldn't sleep all night for reading it, and it's lovely because you put lots of criticism in. That makes it a real biography!' So I knew I was all right.

pause

Now you will hear the piece again. [The piece is repeated.]

pause

That is the end of the test.

Paper 5: Interview (about 15 minutes)

Section A: Picture Conversation (about 5 minutes)

Ask candidates to look at one of the photographs shown below. The first is number 5 and the second number 6 among the Interview Exercises at the back of the Student's Book. Each candidate is assessed for **fluency** and **grammatical accuracy** according to the scales shown on page 12.

5

What's happening in the picture?
Describe each of the men.
What does each man seem to be holding?
Who is the younger man talking to?
Would you stop and listen to him if you were there?

The conversation should lead on to an informal discussion of one or more of the following subjects:

Public speakers; politics and politicians; religion and ethics.

Questions like the following may help to lead the conversation in the right direction:

How seriously do you take public speakers like the younger man?
Do you take a great interest in politics?
Do you trust politicians?
What do *you* think are the 'three basic problems' of society today?
What kinds of things do you think are 'sinful' or 'wrong'?

6

What's happening in the picture?
What kind of people are they?
Where do you think the photo was taken?
What do you think the woman is thinking?
Would you like to be there yourself?

The conversation should lead on to an informal discussion of one or more of the following subjects:

Open-air events; circuses and funfairs; entertainments.

Questions like the following may help to lead the conversation in the right direction:

What sort of open-air events do you enjoy?
Have you been to a circus or a funfair recently? What did you think of it?
Are circuses cruel to animals?
What kinds of public entertainment do you go to? And what kinds do you avoid?

Section B: Reading Passage (about 3 minutes)

Ask candidates to look at reading passage 15 or 16 among the Interview Exercises at the back of the Student's Book. Ask candidates to identify the possible source of the passage and its subject matter before they read it aloud.

15 Within an hour of landing at the airport I was in a rickety old bus travelling across the delta. The journey took an hour and a half but the fare was the price of a sandwich and a cup of coffee back in New York. This trifling sum transported me, not just to another place but to another age; to a city that was old when our history was just beginning.

16 Do you think teachers and educational authorities have any real understanding of the sort of person the modern world needs? They could within two decades produce a generation that would transform the world. Their ideal of character is one that is completely anarchic. They admire most the sort of personality which would be most suitable for leading a gang of pirates.

Each candidate's **pronunciation** and **stress and rhythm** are assessed according to the scales on page 12.

Section C: Structured Communication Activity (about 5 minutes)

In this section, each candidate's **vocabulary** and **communicative ability** are assessed according to the scales on page 13.

First Communication Activity

Candidate A should look at Interview Exercise 25, candidate B at 33 and candidate C at 41. (This activity is not designed to work as a one-to-one activity.)

Each participant receives information about the proposal to build a bypass round a congested small town. Each then plays a different role, representing a different member of the community, in a discussion of the pros and cons of building the new road.

Allow candidates one or two minutes to prepare for the role-play. Then ask each to outline his or her points of view before a free-for-all discussion. If appropriate, the examiner can play the role of an uninformed and uninvolved visitor to the town to whom the participants give their views and argue their cases.

Second Communication Activity

All candidates should look at Interview Exercise 36.

36

> # The price was £12,000

Imagine that the above sentence is the headline of a news report *or* the last line of a short story. You have a few moments to think of *your* version of the story before you tell it to your group (or to the examiner). You may make some brief notes if you wish to help you remember the story you are going to tell.

Listen to and comment on the other candidates' versions of the story and ask them questions too, if you wish.

Allow one or two minutes preparation time before asking candidates to give their versions of the story. Encourage questions and subsequent discussion of the different stories, allowing friendly criticism of each. Less imaginative candidates may need a hint that the story could be about overcharging, blackmail or kidnapping, for example. If there is insufficient material to sustain the discussion, ask candidates to speculate how their stories would have been different if the price had been £12 instead of £12,000.

Third Communication Activity (Optional reading)

For this sample activity, candidates should look at Interview Exercise 37.

37   What insights does the text you have read give you into the life and character of the writer's country and into the period he or she is writing about?
What relevance does the text have to present-day concerns and interests?

Allow one or two minutes preparation time before asking each candidate to make a statement of his or her views. Encourage candidates to give examples from the text. Ask candidates to comment on each other's contributions and then discuss the topic informally. If there is insufficient material to sustain the discussion, ask candidates to speculate on the question: 'If a modern version of the same story were to be written, how would it be different from the text you have read?'

Practice Test 4

Paper 1: Reading Comprehension (1 hour)

Section A   One mark for each correct answer

1 D	6 D	11 B	16 B	21 B
2 C	7 D	12 A	17 A	22 D
3 C	8 B	13 B	18 A	23 C
4 A	9 D	14 D	19 A	24 D
5 B	10 B	15 B	20 B	25 B

Section B   Two marks for each correct answer

26 C	32 B	36 C
27 B	33 A	37 A
28 B	34 D	38 B
29 D	35 C	39 C
30 C		40 B
31 A		

Total: 55

Paper 2: Composition (2 hours)

Give each composition a mark out of 20, according to the scale shown on page 4. If necessary, look at the sample compositions on pages 5–9 for further guidance on the standards required at each grade in the marking scheme.

Total: 40

Paper 3: Use of English (2 hours)

Section A

Question 1

Deduct the total number of *incorrect* items from 10. Correct spelling is essential.

1 should/must/can	11 in
2 else	12 when/where
3 to	13 as/so
4 not	14 goes/extends/holds
5 at	15 of
6 whose	16 in/inside
7 for	17 even/perhaps/maybe/just/merely/only
8 they	18 without
9 to	19 dash/rush/dive
10 other/successful	20 burned/burnt/injured/hurt

Total: 10

Question 2

Give one mark for each word or phrase between the vertical lines. Ignore the words printed in italics.

a) *They had* | such a fierce dog | *that nobody would visit them.*
             | so fierce a dog |

b) *I can barely* | see   any mark(s) | *on that dress.*
             | make out the mark(s) |
             | distinguish a mark |

c) *Nothing but* | a full apology   would satisfy him.
                      was good enough for him.
                      would do for him.
                      was acceptable to him. |

d) *He didn't* | forget | *and* | neither did she. |
                  | nor did she. |

e) *The moment* | I got up to dance   the band stopped playing. |
              | I decided to get up and dance the band decided to stop playing. |

f) *The doctor suggested (that)* | I should rest. |
                          | I rest. |

g) *Only after a* | twelve-hour wait | did their flight leave. |
              | delay of twelve hours |

h) *They are* | being made to study hard by their teacher. |
         | (being) forced to study hard by their teacher. |

i) *They certainly lived* | (fully) up to our expectations. |

j) *Much* | as I admire his courage | *I think he is foolish.*

Total: 12

Question 3

Give one mark for each word or phrase between the vertical lines. Ignore the words printed in italics.

a) *You* | could have | had a lift in | *my car.*
come with me in
gone with me in
taken
borrowed
used
| gone in |

b) *He must* | have been doing | *at least 90 m.p.h.*
have been going at
have been driving at |

c) *He prefers* | having | it done | *by a mechanic.*
getting | it fixed
to have | it seen to
to get | it repaired |

d) *Aren't you* | supposed to be | *at work today?*
| meant to be |

e) *Had I known you were coming, I* | would have | made | *something for you to eat.*
| 'd have | cooked
prepared
bought
| got |

f) *Clever* | as/though he is | *he still wasn't able to find a solution to the problem.*
as/though he was
as/though he may be |

g) *I wish you* | were coming/going | *with us to Greece.*
would come
could come |

h) *There you are! I* | 've been | looking for | *you everywhere.*
| have been | trying to find |

Total: 12

Question 4

Give one mark for each word or phrase between the vertical lines. Ignore the words printed in italics.

a) | How do you account for | *the difference between the two witnesses' stories?*

b) | He is by no means stupid. |
    | By no means is he stupid. |
    | He isn't stupid by any means. |

c) | 'You take me for granted,' she complained. |
    | She complained that he took her for granted. |
    | She complained that she was being taken for granted. |

d) | Once the giant was dead | *they lived in peace.*
    | Once the giant had died |
    | Once the giant died |

e) *The man in that painting* | reminds me very much of | *my uncle.*

f) | She has had | her bicycle stolen. |

g) | They were known to be | *spies.*
    | It was known that they were |

h) | I came across it | *when I was looking through some old papers.*
    | I came upon it |
    | It came to light |

i) *We didn't go* | for fear of being | *recognised.*
              | for fear we were |
              | for fear we might be |
    | The fear of being recognised prevented us from going. |

j) *After two hours* | there was still no sign | of the bridegroom. |
                 | there still wasn't any sign |

Total: 12

Section B

Question 5

Give the marks shown for each question for coherent and relevant answers.

a)	The parts where the cooking, etc. is done. (NOT dining room/reception)	1
b)	Work with a *regular* pace and character.	1
c)	The chaos.	1
d)	That the workload and its timing are unpredictable.	2
e)	Doing two men's work.	1
f)	The quarrels kept them up to the right intensity (1) by spurring each other on (1).	2
g)	The staff keep each other up to the mark (1), and so keep the hotel going (1).	2

h) Establishes or ruins   1

i) With deliberate rudeness (insults) (2) except to the head waiter (1).
(feelings – superiority, authority, etc. only = 1)   3

j) One mark for clear expression of each of the following points:
– receiving orders for dishes
– giving detailed instructions
– inspecting   4
– taking responsibility for timing (NOT just 'different times', etc.)

k) Women are no less skilful than men (1) but not as good at the strict timing
needed (1).
(NOT straight quotes on men as cooks)   2

l) Indirectly, with someone else actually doing it. (clear definitions – 'identifies with rich
customers', etc. – not enough)   2

m) They cannot save (1) enough to escape (1).   2

n) One mark each for the following 7 points, plus 3 marks on impression for relevance,
conciseness and accuracy:
Cooks – most pride in job skill
        – awareness of position
Waiters – identify with customers
        – no objection to being servile
        – proud of job skill
Plongeurs – no pride in job as such
        – proud of ability to do hard work   10

Total: 34

Paper 4: Listening Comprehension (31 minutes)

First Part: Tattooing

        Score
1 A   1
2 A   1
3 C   1
4 A   1
5 C   1
6 D   1

Total: 6 marks

Second Part: Phobias

Score

7 C 1
8 A 1
9 C 1

Total: 3 marks

Third Part: Glass bottles

Score

10 basic ingredients [✓] ½
    labour [ ] ½
    fuel [✓] ½
    advertising [ ] ½

½ mark for each box correctly ticked or left unticked. ½ mark off for each box incorrectly ticked.

11 more attractive [✓] ½
    more exact size [✓] ½
    heavier [ ] ½
    thicker [ ] ½

½ mark for each box correctly ticked or left unticked. ½ mark off for each box incorrectly ticked.

12 A 1
13 D 1

Total: 6 marks

Fourth Part: Weather forecast

14   *Score*

	This afternoon	Tonight	Tomorrow	Tomorrow night	
over 5°C					
0°C–5°C	✓				1
below 0°C (frost)		✓		✓	2
below −5°C (heavy frost)					

One mark for each box correctly ticked.

15

colder than inland		½
warmer than inland	✓	½
windier than inland	✓	½
less windy than inland		½

½ mark for each box correctly ticked or left unticked. Deduct ½ mark for each box incorrectly ticked.

Total: 5 marks

Transcript

University of Cambridge Local Examination Syndicate. This is the Certificate of Proficiency in English Listening Comprehension Test.
Test Number Four
For the first part of the test you will hear a radio interview about tattooing. Look at questions 1–6. For questions 1 to 6 tick one of the boxes A, B, C or D. You will hear the piece twice.

pause

TATTOOING

Presenter: Now, you may have noticed that lots of people, including women, who aren't traditional tattoo material, are these days having their bodies decorated with brightly coloured butterflies or orchids or fish. Gone are the days of black and blue anchors on large hairy arms only. Ron Aldridge has been looking at tattoos and he began his investigation in a tattooist's parlour in North London.

Ron Aldridge: Playing fly on the wall in a parlour which felt a little like an informal dentist's surgery, I watched as the 9 by 4 inch design was started. As the needle went to work, Dick gave me a guided tour of his chest and arms.

Dick: I have got a sort of sequence. If you look at . . look at me, the . . er . . left arm – the lower arm for instance has three dragons on and the lower right arm has . . er . . three birds, various kinds of birds, that, well, two ea . . er . . a . . a double eagle and two different kinds of birds of paradise I suppose is the best way of describing them. And . . um . . the upper left arm for instance in a way counter-balances the upper right arm, it has a hawk on the top instead of a . . bat. But it has a lion's head where this one has a . . a rather stylised tiger's head.

Ron Aldridge: Which all in all totalled 15 tattoos, but as the beads of blood appeared, I had to ask: 'Does it hurt?'

Dick: You feel just a slight sharpness initially, er . . but it's really very low, it's for instance not as severe as if a cat scratched you. If a cat scratched you you'd probably, well, you certainly would notice it far more. The reason

69

there I think simply that the cat doesn't just . . er . . puncture four layers of skin of course, it goes right through and draws a lot of blood.

Ron Aldridge: Though of course a cat scratch is quick and inadvertent. Perhaps Dick is particularly thick-skinned. Certainly everyone else I talked to was rather more impressed with the pain and apparently if you sob your way through the entire experience the tattooist forgets the charge. In effect, of course, tattooing is just another form of beautification, colouring of the body and that we almost all indulge in in one form or another, we always have. But a tattoo is permanent, you might have to live with it for 40 years.

pause

Now you will hear the piece again. [The piece is repeated.]

pause

That is the end of the first part of the test.

Second Part
For the second part of the test you will hear an interview with a doctor. Look at questions 7–9. For each question tick one of the boxes A, B, C or D. You will hear the piece twice.

pause

PHOBIAS

Presenter: How many people then, do you think are affected by phobias?
Doctor: Well, there . . there would be thousands, and . . er . . a lot of people keep these quiet, and they stay indoors and . . and don't talk to anybody about it. They're often frightened, what one would call a sort of secondary anxiety, that people are going to laugh at them, and scorn them for having the fear.
  Now, if I think . . er . . what was the last thing that I was frightened of this morning? A wasp flew into my car and I stopped and I got out quick, and had I not been panicking, and had I slowed down a bit I . . I wouldn't have risked the traffic coming up behind and so on. I . . I was trying to keep the thing under control, that's a very everyday experience.
Presenter: So you're saying really then, that we've all got little phobias I suppose, I mean . . um . . like spiders and what have you, things like that?
Doctor: Little bits of panic, and the essential of the experience of a phobia, can be that you can have great peaks of panic with it. The panic comes on in an overwhelming way and absolutely dominates the body functions, you may start sweating and blushing and shaking, and when it feels like that, one is absolutely disabled for the duration of the panic.
Presenter: Can these phobias suddenly develop, I mean, literally overnight?
Doctor: People do describe this, but on the whole the sort of person who's going to develop phobias is a person who is very sensitive. Now I mean that in the nicest possible way, a sensitive person, also a person who conditions very easily. Now, if . . if I could just explain what I mean by that. If you, for instance, work in a cold storage, what you don't know is going on, is that on your way to the job all your skin blood vessels are shutting down, and when you get into the front door they shut down a little bit more, when you draw on your special cold-proof clothing the skin vessels shut down even more.

And this is just an example of how the body conditions itself before an event to what it needs to be doing.

Now, some people condition very much more rapidly, and they condition to fears and to rather frightening or socially worrying experiences and of course one aspect of the phobias is that there is very often a . . a big . . a big social component in it, that one's frightful, frightened of what people are going to think of you. I said frightful, people are going to say, 'Look at this frightful person! Here they come, coming along,' and one gets fears of meeting people.

Presenter: Are some of them very, very unusual indeed though, really irrational.

Doctor: Well, you can usually find some spark of rationality in most phobias. The obvious ones are travel, airlines. I was quite frightened of the high-speed train when I first sat in it, I remember. And then I remembered that Queen Victoria, or somebody like that, sat in the first trains that were going at about 25 miles per hour, and . . and she feared that the wheels would fly off and the thing would crash.

You can usually find some element of it, and . . and if a person is able to remember back into their childhood, they can very often remember an incident which helps to explain why they're frightened of that particular thing.

pause

Now you will hear the piece again. [The piece is repeated.]

pause

That is the end of the second part of the test.

Third Part

For the third part of the test you will hear part of a programme about the manufacture of glass bottles. Look at questions 10–13. For questions 10 and 11 tick the appropriate boxes. For questions 12 and 13 tick one of the boxes A, B, C or D. You will hear the piece twice.

pause

GLASS BOTTLES

Reporter: Have you noticed? Bottles are getting thinner. Actually it's not the bottles themselves, but the glass walls of the bottles. There are several reasons for this. The raw materials from which glass is made are becoming, like everything else, very expensive. A continuing energy crisis puts up the manufacturing costs. And last but by no means least bottles are in greater competition today with lightweight aluminium cans and plastic containers. All this means more modern and efficient systems in the manufacturing process. I've recently been to visit Rockware Glass in the Yorkshire city of Doncaster. It's a factory which specialises mainly in glass containers for the food industry. They range from the traditional narrow-necked bottles you put sauces and ketchup in to the wide-necked jars for jams and fruit juices. David Pearson is the Production Director at Rockware Glass.

Mr Pearson: What we're trying to produce is something which will show off the . . the product . . um . . to the public with good effect; a lightweight container which doesn't feel too heavy to carry around, and one which is sufficiently strong to withstand the knocking and bashing around in . . in service. It's . . it's as simple as that really.

Reporter: I suppose the actual dimensions of the bottle in lots of applications are very important?

Mr Pearson: Um . . all dimensions of bottles are becoming more and more . . um . . important, particularly with respect to automatic filling lines where outside tolerances do not allow the bottle to go down the line. Er . . so we work to very very tight tolerances on specification.

Reporter: The basic ingredients of glass are sand, limestone and soda ash. Very small quantities of other chemicals are sometimes added to change the colour or to make one of those opaque glasses. Once the type of glass has been decided on the production process can begin.

Mr Pearson: The first thing to do is to mix the ingredients together thoroughly in order that you have no inhomogeneity coming through into the glass eventually. So it's a thorough mixing of all the raw materials in lots of about four to five tons per time. This is automatic on call from level bindicators at the furnace platform area.

Reporter: What does that mean exactly?

Mr Pearson: It means that when the . . our furnace is running short of components for . . er . . melting glass it will call for . . from the batch plant for a new supply which will trigger automatically the mixing cycle and will then transfer the materials to the waiting bin. The bin then fills up to a level where yet another indicator will indicate that the bin is full and the whole process stops; this then waits until the . . bin is depleted and the whole cycle starts again.

Reporter: So when the ingredients are mixed it's, what, tipped straight into the furnace?

Mr Pearson: No. When the ingredients are mixed they are transferred something like 150 metres along conveyors into the . . er . . storage bins, where then transferred into the furnace via special batch-charging machines which allow the level of glass in the furnace to be maintained at a very constant rate.

Reporter: And how are the mixed ingredients actually pushed into the machine when required?

Mr Pearson: Um . . the mixed ingredients are . . are pushed into the furnace, or should I say transferred into the furnace, by a variety of means. Er..some methods rely directly upon gravity, others rely on being pushed into the furnace, and others are vibrated. You'll see a mixture of all three in this particular factory. But then the . . the glass, on transfer into the furnace, is heated up to about 1,550 degrees Centigrade . . um . . before being cooled off to about 1,250 degrees Centigrade before transferring into the bottle-making machine.

Reporter: So, in other words, it has to be heated to a higher temperature in order to make it, if you like, than the temperature at which you work with it?

Mr Pearson: Yes. The . . the reason for that is it is important to get out all impurities like . . er . . pieces of unmelted batch components . . er . . drive off the . . um . . little bubbles of air which are produced during melting – we call this seed, by the way um . . in order to give a glass which is clear and without blemishes when it is finally made into a bottle.

Reporter: At this stage of my visit to Rockware Glass I felt it was time to see for myself some of the processes that David Pearson and Albert Hill had described. So, accompanied by technical officer, Ian Wilson, I began at the beginning – the huge tower – the Batch Plant – where the ingredients are mixed.

Mr Wilson:	Right at the top of the tower are large containers for the raw materials. Half way down is a mixing plant . . er . . where all the units are weighed out . . um . . fairly accurately to within about half a kilo, and then . . er . . down at the bottom of the tower is . . er . . something similar to a big cement mixer that just mixes all the materials together.
Reporter:	And then when it's all mixed up how is it sent into the factory to the furnaces?
Mr Wilson:	Er . . it's taken back up through a bucket elevator into three separate conveyor belts, one going to each furnace.
Reporter:	We moved on into the factory itself and there, in a relatively quiet corner, was a computer associated with the furnaces. Furnace Foreman Jim Ayre, looks after it.
Mr Ayre:	What it does is it monitors the furnace as it's running and it will go around the furnace and monitor the temperatures and the firing mould and all the positions of . . er . . the equipment at that particular time. If something is wrong then it will alarm and tell us that there's a fault wherever and we can go straight to it.
Reporter:	And it'll give you some indication of what the fault is, will it?
Mr Ayre:	That's correct, yeah.
Reporter:	The next port of call in my tour was the noisiest part of the factory. Right next door to the furnace and above the gob machine. It was also very hot . . .

pause

Now you will hear the piece again. [The piece is repeated.]

pause

That is the end of the third part of the test.

Fourth Part
For the fourth part you will hear a weather report. Look at questions 14 and 15. For question 14 you will need to tick one box for each period. For question 15 you will need to tick two of the boxes. You will hear the piece twice.

pause

WEATHER FORECAST

This is the weatherline service for East Anglia covering Cambridgeshire, Norfolk and Suffolk.

Here is the forecast for East Anglia valid until 6.00 a.m. tomorrow. Issued at noon on Friday 18th of February.

This afternoon will be dry and sunny but still rather cold, temperatures only rising to five degrees Centigrade.

This evening and overnight there will be clear skies. Temperatures will fall quickly, reaching a minimum of minus 5 degrees inland, giving a moderate frost. However near the coast with the continuing light to force three east to north-east wind, temperatures will be nearer zero degrees Centigrade.

Near coastal waters winds will be easterly force four. The outlook for the following 24 hours: little change, dry and fine by day but rather cold with night frost. Thank you for calling.

pause

Now you will hear the piece again. [The piece is repeated.]

pause

That is the end of the test.

Paper 5: Interview (about 15 minutes)

Section A: Picture Conversation (about 5 minutes)

Ask candidates to look at one of the photographs shown below. The first is number 7 and the second number 8 among the Interview Exercises at the back of the Student's Book. Each candidate is assessed for **fluency** and **grammatical accuracy** according to the scales shown on page 12.

7

What's happening in this picture?
What kind of people are they?
How well do you think they know each other?
What do you think they are saying to each other?
Where do you think the photo was taken?
How would you feel if you were the lady on the right?

The conversation should lead on to an informal discussion of one or more of the following subjects:

Pets; hygiene and public health; clothes.

Questions like the following may help to lead the conversation in the right direction:

Do you have any pets?
What do you think of people who love their pets very much?
Are dogs a public nuisance and health hazard?
Are people in general too fanatical about hygiene and keeping healthy?
What do you think of the clothes the ladies are wearing?
Do you prefer your clothes to be comfortable or smart?

What's happening in this picture?
Describe each of the runners you can see.
What kind of people take part in races like this?
Would you ever take part in such a race?

The conversation should lead on to an informal discussion of one or more of the following subjects:

Keeping fit; getting older; sports.

Questions like the following may help to lead the conversation in the right direction:

How do you try to keep fit?
Are the runners in the photo too old to be competing?
Are you worried about getting old?
What sports do you enjoy participating in and which do you enjoy watching?
How important is sport in your life?
Describe the most popular sport in your country.

Section B: Reading Passage (about 3 minutes)

Ask candidates to look at reading passage 17 or 18 among the Interview Exercises at the back of the Student's Book. Ask them to identify the possible source of the passage and its subject matter before reading it aloud.

17 Your Snack'n'Sandwich Toaster will quickly become an indispensable family asset, because its quality and sensible design features always result in a superb product. The toaster is designed to seal and cut your sandwiches in half automatically. You may care to notice the thermostat control, which not only saves you money but also gives golden brown sandwiches every time.

18 The sixties really were a phenomenal help to all of us, but they really followed, I think, the social revolution of the fifties when dramatists and other writers were actually changing the words that people were saying in the theatre and in the street. Then of course in the sixties youngsters for the first time had money. Physically things had changed.

Each candidate's **pronunciation** and **stress and rhythm** are assessed according to the scales on page 12.

Section C: Structured Communication Activity (about 5 minutes)

In this section, each candidate's **vocabulary** and **communicative ability** are assessed according to the scales on page 13.

First Communication Activity

Candidate A should look at Interview Exercise 26, candidate B at 34 and candidate C at 42. (In a one-to-one interview the examiner may look at candidate's C's information and the single candidate see both A and B's information.)

Each candidate has a reproduction of an intriguing painting. The task is to describe the painting they have before them to the others and, later, to look at all three and discuss what they find interesting, appealing or displeasing about them.

Allow one or two minutes for candidates to study their pictures and prepare their descriptions. Then get each candidate to describe his or her picture without allowing the others to see it; encourage the others to ask any questions they wish that help them to build up a complete mental picture of what is being described. When everyone has finished, allow them to see each other's pictures and comment in a friendly way on the descriptions they heard. Then they should discuss what they like or find interesting about the three paintings. If there is insufficient material to sustain the discussion, ask the candidates to describe another painting they like very much and, perhaps, to talk about the last time they visited an art gallery (or to say why they never do) and the kind of paintings they like.

(No special artistic knowledge is required for this activity. Indeed, if any candidate seems to be dominating the conversation with his or her enthusiasm or expertise, make sure the others have a chance to express the layman's, or even philistine's, view!)

Second Communication Activity
All candidates should look at Interview Exercise 44.

44 Imagine that you have to describe the modern world to someone who has just been rescued after being alone on a desert island for the last fifty years. Decide with your partners how you would describe
either TV and video
or modern aircraft and airports.

Imagine that the person you will be talking to is going to use video equipment (or travel by plane and use airport facilities). You do not need to be an expert on either topic to be able to talk about it.

Allow the group to decide first which of the topics they wish to talk about and allow a minute or two for preparation. Then chair the discussion or, if you prefer, play the role of the returned castaway and ask the candidates to describe the ideas to you. Encourage candidates to work together and to pool their knowledge and experience. If by any chance the chosen topic does not provide enough material, ask candidates to explain what else is different about the modern world, compared to the world the castaway remembers.

Third Communication Activity (optional reading)
For this sample exercise, candidates should look at Interview Exercise 45.

45 How is the text you have read typical of its *genre* (tragedy, historical novel, short story collection, etc.)?
How does it stand out as an exceptional example of the *genre* and what makes it particularly 'special' or 'great'?
What ideas do you think the writer is trying to get across in this particular story (or collection)?

Allow one to two minutes preparation time before asking each candidate to make a statement of his or her views, giving examples from the text. Then encourage comments on each contribution before an informal discussion of the points raised. If there is insufficient material to sustain the discussion, ask candidates to discuss what the main themes of the text are and what 'message' the writer is trying to put across.

Practice Test 5

Paper 1: Reading Comprehension (1 hour)

Section A   One mark for each correct answer

1 C	6 A	11 A	16 D	21 D
2 A	7 A	12 D	17 C	22 B
3 B	8 A	13 D	18 C	23 A
4 B	9 C	14 A	19 A	24 B
5 C	10 A	15 C	20 A	25 A

Section B   Two marks for each correct answer

26 D	31 D	36 C
27 B	32 C	37 D
28 B	33 B	38 A
29 A	34 D	39 D
30 D	35 B	40 B

Total: 55

Paper 2: Composition (2 hours)

Give each composition a mark out of 20, according to the scale shown on page 4. If necessary, look at the sample compositions on pages 5–9 for further guidance on the standards required at each grade in the marking scheme.

Total: 40

Paper 3: Use of English (2 hours)

Section A

Question 1

Deduct the total number of *incorrect* items from 10. Correct spelling is essential.

1 Whether	11 of
2 makes	12 for
3 not	13 But/However/Yet/Nevertheless/Nonetheless/Unfortunately
4 put	14 enable/help/allow/permit/aid/assist
5 in	15 more
6 the	16 most/many/highly/regrettably, etc.
7 union	17 of/in
8 and	18 make/impose/place
9 on/upon	19 of
10 free/liberate/release	20 to

Total: 10

Question 2

Give one mark for each word or phrase between the vertical lines. Ignore the words printed in italics.

a) *I'd rather* | you didn't smoke | *in here.*
  you did not smoke
  you refrained from smoking |

b) *Try as hard* | as I might I | *couldn't open the door.*

c) *Her performance made* | a considerable impression | on (the) critics. |
  a great impression
  a favourable impression
  a remarkable impression |

d) *It's high time something* | was/were done about the city's traffic problems | *by the
                                                                                    council.*

e) *Only later* | did I realise/realize who he was. |

f) *There has* | been | a considerable fall | in the value | *of sterling in the past
                a sharp   drop   week.*
                a substantial   decrease |
                                decline |

g) *We'll still go* | even if it rains. |
  whether or not it rains.
  whether it rains or not. |

h) *So as* | not to disturb | *the children, we left quietly.*
  to avoid disturbing |

i) *There's* | nothing | (that) I wouldn't/would not do for you. |

j) *If you had told me* | in advance | *I could have avoided that date.*
| in (good) time |
| earlier (than this/you did) |
| before (this/you did) |
| beforehand |

Total: 14

Question 3

Give one mark for each word or phrase between the vertical lines. Ignore the words printed in italics.

a) *Our dog was so ill that we* | had | him | *put down by the vet.*
| had to have | her |
| were going to have | it |

b) *Once he's been there a few weeks, Richard* | will | have got | *used to his*
| should | have become | *new school.*
	be getting
	get
	become

c) *My uncle's been dead for years. You* | couldn't have | *seen him yesterday.*
| couldn't possibly have |
| can't have |
| can't possibly have |

d) *I don't believe you.* | Let me | *see you lift that suitcase.*
| I'd like to |

e) *I shall resign* | if you refuse to | *accept my proposal.*
| if they refuse to |
| if the manager, *etc.* refuses to |
| unless I can persuade them to |

f) *The plane was due at 9.45. It* | should have | *landed by now.*
| ought to have |
| will have |
| must have |
| is sure to have |
| is bound to have |

g) *Listening to the radio is a good way of* | keeping | *yourself informed about current affairs.*

h) *In spite* | of missing | *the bus he still arrived on time.*
| of being late for |
| of the slowness, *etc.* of |

i) *If you had been in that situation,* | what action | would you have | *taken?*
what decision
what steps
what precautions
how long

Total: 12

Question 4

Give one mark for each word or phrase between the vertical lines. Ignore the words printed in italics.

a) *We* | could (just) make out the buildings | *through the fog.*
could (just) make the buildings out
were (just) able to make out the buildings

b) *I* | strongly | suspect that John was | *responsible.*
suspect John of being
suspect John of having been

c) | He gets on (well) with | *all his students.*
He gets along (well) with

d) | I can't/won't put up with his rude behaviour.
His rude behaviour (has) put me off.

e) | A lot of people turned out/up for the meeting.
A large number (of people) turned up/out for the meeting.

f) | The old house had seen/known better days. |

g) *As a boy,* | he used to | go to church regularly.
be a regular churchgoer.

h) | What are her chances of passing | *the exam?*
What are the chances of her passing

i) | The film fell short of my expectations. |

j) | I have had enough of | *that dreadful noise.*

Total: 12

Section B

Question 5

Give the marks shown for each question for coherent and relevant answers.

a) Studying/discovering archaeological sites (1) through photographs taken from the air (1).   2

b) The total pattern (view, etc.) is not perceived from too close a viewpoint. (difference of viewpoint only = 1)   2

c) Being able to see the total pattern from a height. (mention of 'carpets' = 0)   1

d) Complete/all-inclusive, etc.   1

e) Because of ploughing.   1

f) The sun is near the horizon/rising/setting sun (1) and it casts (longer) shadows (1).   2

g) Crops growing better/faster, etc. in some places than in others (1). This is caused by differing depth of soil (1) over underlying features (walls, ditches, etc.) (1).   3

h) (Buried) walls, (filled-in) ditches. (both essential for mark)   1

i) Obvious/evident, etc. (NOT 'distinguished', 'noticed', 'indicated', etc.)   1

j) Aerial photography.   1

k) The crop with deep roots owing to the deep soil over filled-in ditches will turn yellow later/remain green longer. ('The converse is also true', etc. or example unrelated to text = 1)   2

l) When the crops colour/ripen/become parched (2). The right season (NOT time of day) (1).   3

m) Underlying features/crop with shallow/deep roots/differential growth.   1

n) They are formed by ploughing, which shows colour differences.   1

o) Impression mark out of maximum of/10 (taking broad standard Poor 2, Adequate 5, Good 8), rewarding positively conciseness and good expression with inclusion of the following points:
–they give a comprehensive view of archaeological features
–they reveal features hidden from ground
–by shadows/crop marks/soil marks
(penalise lifting)   10

Total: 32

Paper 4: Listening Comprehension (32 minutes)

First Part: Earthquake

		Score
1	True	½
2	True	½
3	False	½
4	False	½
5	True	½
6	False	½
7	False	½
8	False	½
9	True	½
10	False	½

Total: 5 marks

Second Part: Taking cuttings

11 Tick **only** in **box 3** = 4 marks. (One mark for each box correctly ticked or left
    unticked. Deduct one mark for each box incorrectly ticked or incorrectly left unticked.)

Total: 4 marks

Third Part: Food processing in Sri Lanka

		Score
12	D	1
13	B	1
14	A	1
15	A	1
16	B	1
17	B	1

Total: 6 marks

Fourth Part: Micro-computers

		Score
18	C	1
19	A	1
20	D	1
21	A	1
22	C	1

Total: 5 marks

Transcript

*University of Cambridge Local Examinations Syndicate. This is the Certificate of Proficiency in
English Listening Comprehension Test.*
Test Number Five
*For the first part of the test you will hear part of a radio news programme about an earthquake.
Look at questions 1–10. For each of the questions tick whether the statements are true or false.
You will hear the piece twice.*

pause

EARTHQUAKE

In Mexico a powerful earthquake rocked the southern part of the country and caused
damage to buildings and an electricity blackout in part of the capital, Mexico City.
Although there were no immediate reports of injuries, correspondents say the tremor
registered the same strength as the one in the Mexican State of Oaxaca a year ago when
65 people died. Electricity failure in the latest earthquake caused a breakdown in the
Mexico City underground railway and thousands of passengers were trapped for a short
time. The tremor was felt at the resort of Cancun where leaders of 22 nations had ended
their discussions on bridging the gap between the world's rich and poor nations. Two of

83

the leaders, the British Prime Minister, Mrs Thatcher, and the Chinese Premier, Deng Xiaoping, are now in Mexico City for talks with President Lopez Portillo.

pause

Now you will hear the piece again. [The piece is repeated.]

pause

That is the end of the first part of the test.

Second Part
For the second part of the test you will hear a gardening expert explaining how to take cuttings. Look at question 11. Tick the appropriate boxes labelled 1, 2, 3 and 4. You will hear the piece twice.

pause

TAKING CUTTINGS

Presenter: Well, September is upon us–a busy month for the gardener. And it's an expensive month too. So if you're counting the pennies here's some advice from Michael Lidstone on the topic of re-stocking the garden. He showed Ann Thompson how to avoid the need to buy rose bushes by taking cuttings from existing ones.

Ann: I always seem to be interrupting you when you're doing hard work Michael, but . . er . . is September really a good month to take cuttings of roses?

Michael: Well, September's the best month, Ann, because you don't need to protect them at all. You don't need a greenhouse or even a cold-frame. All you need is a bit of reasonably worked soil.

Ann: What exactly is a cutting, Michael?

Michael: Ah, yes. What is a cutting? Well, basically, Ann, a cutting is just a piece cut out of a plant and stuck in the ground to form roots and develop into a new plant.

Ann: Mm, well, I suppose the most important part of it all is . . is your original choice of the cutting. Er . . what do you look for on the main bush?

Michael: That's it. That's very important. On the main bush the . . er . . wood to look for is a fairly strong young branch . . er . . like this one. Down here we can see there's a fairly good one–and a quick snip! Now, er . . there's a nice shoot that's about as thick as a pencil. And it's . . er . . thickening up a bit so it's becoming quite firm.

Ann: Now, I notice you've gone for a cutting that doesn't have any flowers on it. Is that right?

Michael: That's a good idea, yes. Because flowering shoots are busily concentrating on flowering. If you can get one where the flowers have faded that's a good sort to choose, because you can just snip off the dead bloom at the top . . er . . like that! And you've got . . er . . well, there you are, your pencil thickness and a good shoot that's finished flowering and can concentrate on getting some roots formed now.

Ann: I guess that's what we've got to concentrate on now, to get it to form some roots. Now, how do you go about it?

Michael: Well, take your shoot now, like this one I've got in my hand. And it's almost 18 inches long. So that's going to make two decent cuttings because at this time of the year cuttings want to be about 9 inches long when they're hard wood. So let's start by looking at the top of your shoot and making a clean snip just above a leaf. There! Right above it so there's nothing to die back. The wood will always die back to a leaf.

Ann: What about at the bottom?

Michael: At the bottom, work down as I say about 9 inches, 10 if you like, and then make a cut underneath a leaf.

Ann: Underneath it. Very close to the leaf, I see.

Michael: Yes. Very, very close. So there's a leaf top and bottom and a few in between.

Ann: And I notice you make your cuts straight across and . . and not at an angle.

Michael: That's right. This is after years of trial and error. It's been found to be the best way of doing things. Then all you've got to do is leave the top two leaves and strip all the rest off. So there we are. We've got a rather silly looking thing now–about 9 inches long, firm stem, pencil thickness, two leaves at the top.

Ann: Only two.

Michael: It doesn't need any more to make food. If you leave too many on it's going to sweat. It's going to lose water through them. We want it to get roots out. So by next summer I'll have a new rose bush and it's cost me nothing.

Ann: Aren't you clever! It looks so easy.

Michael: There's nothing to it.

pause

now you will hear the piece again. [The piece is repeated.]

pause

That is the end of the second part of the test.

Third Part

For the third part of the test you will hear a radio programme about food processing. Look at questions 12–17. For each question tick one of the boxes A, B, C or D. You will hear the piece twice.

pause

FOOD PROCESSING IN SRI LANKA

Presenter: One commodity tropical countries tend to be rich in is fruit but it's often not used to its full advantage. Tropical fruits tend to be seasonal and because normally little processing is done it's often sold off too cheap when it's in abundance or left to waste and then there's none available for the rest of the year.

Well, the Sri Lankan development organisation Savodia is setting up an experimental small village food factory which will be one up from a cottage industry. The project's being organised by a food technologist, Nigel Freeman, who's being sponsored by Intermediate Technology Industrial Services, and Annie Allsebrook went to find out about it from him. She joined him in a kitchen at the Savodia headquarters where the first women were being trained in food processing.

Nigel Freeman: We hope there will be about eight women working in it . . er . . it will be to produce food to sell in Savodia village co-operative shops and maybe to sell to the outside market–the tourist trade. And as well it will be a training centre to train women to preserve food in their home.

Annie Allsebrook: At the moment we're in a kitchen at the headquarters of Savodia which is operating as a factory until the factory is actually ready and we're surrounded by bottles, empty beer bottles and . . er . . we've got full jars of jam and all sorts of things. What have we got here and what equipment? What are you doing here?

Nigel Freeman: Er . . at the moment we're just trying to develop a product, product development. So we're trying different recipes, tasting things, seeing how they keep, trying out different packaging. Jam bottles–these are second-hand jam bottles that have been used in the kitchen. We buy new tops. Er . . when we've washed them, we have a small steam generator so we can sterilise them. So at the moment we are just . . er . . trying different recipes, tasting them and showing the girls; I have three women working for me just trying to..er..teach them using different equipment, making sure that they pasteurise it, heat it properly, so that when we make a product they keep, they don't spoil.

Annie Allsebrook: What products have you tried so far?

Nigel Freeman: Things we've tried so far are . . it . . we're dealing with just fruits, so that's lime, pineapple, mangoes, papaya . . er . . wood-apple. We're making . . er . .juices, just juice . . er . . cordials–that's juice with sugar and water, jams . . er . . and pickles.

Annie Allsebrook: Now this factory is going to be in a village, now is it really realistic to have a food processing factory in a village using simple techniques. Isn't there a risk of . . er . . poor hygiene and poor quality produce?

Nigel Freeman: Yeah, this is always a problem but it . . it can be overcome by understanding the problem and knowing the ways of getting round it. The first thing is, we do need clean water. Er . . we are using water out of a drinking well that we shall . . er . . put into a tank to allow the sediment to settle and we shall chlorinate it. Er . . we have it regularly tested in a laboratory in Colombo. Though we have to teach the girls the importance of hygiene, make them wear hats, aprons, make sure there's basins ready available with soap . . er . . teach them the . . each time they go to the toilet they must wash their hands, each time they come into the factory they must clean their hands. They must not eat in the factory, they must not bring animals or smoke cigarettes in the factory. It's basic, simple rules and then hygiene should not be too much of a problem. Then the other side is keeping the factory clean, designing the factory such that it won't harbour rats . . er . . or allow insects to fly in and allow birds to come in. Make sure that the drains do drain, that they are kept clean . . er . . that they do not get blocked . . er . . making sure that the . . the toilets work properly and . . and function and it's just . . er . . basically making sure that simple hygiene is kept up to a certain standard.

Annie Allsebrook: When it gets going properly, how many women do you think will be there and how much processed food will they be producing a week?

Nigel Freeman: Initially we hope that within six months of the factory starting that we shall be employing something like eight women and producing something like a hundred bottles a day: so a hundred bottles of juice or a hundred bottles, a hundred pots of jam in a day. And then if they can do that on a regular basis, producing a product that is of a standard quality that does not vary and there is shown that there is a market then the project might become bigger, they might get more specialised equipment.

Annie Allsebrook: Do you think a similar factory could be set up elsewhere or does it need . . er . . expertise and . . er . . quite a lot of funding?

Nigel Freeman: By the end of a certain period, six months or a year, we would have produced a manual, that had all the information of the construction of the building, the type of equipment needed, the problems that had risen before and we would have trained people who have originally seen all the problems and had developed enough experience to start another factory on their own. The . . the technology required is not that complicated, a lot of it is just mainly organisation, routine, making sure that things are heated to a certain temperature, they are filled into bottles at a certain temperature, the bottles are clean and arranging that they have enough raw material for production on a certain day, that they have bottles, that they have gas, they have electricity, they have enough water. So a lot of it is just making sure that there are enough things in the right place at the right time.

pause

Now you will hear the piece again. [The piece is repeated.]

pause

That is the end of the third part of the test.

Fourth Part
For the fourth part of the test you will hear part of a radio programme about micro-processors. Look at questions 18–22. For questions 18–22 tick one of the boxes A, B, C or D. You will hear the piece twice.

pause

MICRO-COMPUTERS

Rob Berry: The micro-computer world is about to be infested by a plague of mice. Now, fortunately these are friendly creatures and their job is to help computer users find their way through the software jungle. In fact the mice I am talking about are an essential part of a new concept in personal computer systems developed by the Apple Corporation and the way they are used will, I hope, become clear in the next few minutes. The system itself is called LISA, which stands for Local Integrated Software Architecture, and it's the result of more than 200 man years of development. When I visited the Corporation's British headquarters at Hemel Hempstead near London, Brian Reynolds, Personal Office Systems Marketing Manager, told me that in broad terms there are two major differences between LISA and conventional systems.

Brian Reynolds: Firstly in ease of use LISA emulates the way we work and even emulates our desk top so that LISA works the way we do. It is totally simple, you don't have to type in commands to tell the computer what you want to do; you simply point to options, that selects them and the machine does what you've pointed to telling it what to do. The other main area is integration, LISA integrates text data and graphics all in front of the user, this hasn't been possible with computers in the past and it's part of the new technology which Apple has developed.

Rob Berry: As you may have gathered from the background humming noise we were sitting in front of a LISA while we talked and I asked Mike (*sic*) Reynolds to describe what we could see.

Brian Reynolds: Basically it's a box with a screen on it . . um . . it has a keyboard in front of it so that you can type information into it, for example if you were going to type a letter. Beside that box there is a small device called a Mouse. This is a very small box about the size of a packet of cigarettes and you can move this around on your desk top–it has one key on it. As you move it around on your desk top a pointer on the screen moves around also pointing to pictures of objects typically that you would find around in your office; for example, a calculator, a waste bin, a filing cabinet. If I pointed it to the filing cabinet and pressed the button on the Mouse it opens the filing cabinet. If I point it to the calculator by pointing to one of the pictures of buttons on the calculator on the screen and pressing the button on the Mouse, I'm actually pressing a button on the calculator on the screen which really means I'd do it the same way as I'd..I would normally use a calculator but it's never been possible to do that before.

I never ever look at the Mouse of course, I always look at the desk top, the graphical representation of a desk top which is the screen, and I look at the little arrow on the screen. As I move the Mouse the little arrow moves. If I move the Mouse up the arrow moves up, if I move it down similarly it moves down and sideways the same. So . . the . . the arrow really represents everything I do with my hand happens on . . on the screen. The Mouse is connected to the computer by a very, very thin cord and that goes into the computer and the computer then senses what the Mouse is doing. The Mouse actually has a very small little ball in the bottom of it–I'll take it out and show it to you–there it is a li . . a little ball and that rolls around inside the Mouse on your desk top so it tells the computer where the Mouse is on the desk top.

Rob Berry: So it doesn't have to be on a special surface, it can be any surface at all?

Brian Reynolds: Absolutely, absolutely not, it can work on absolutely any surface, any desk top it's designed to work on. It would even work on my lap if I put it there.

pause

Now you will hear the piece again. [The piece is repeated.]

pause

That is the end of the test.

Paper 5: Interview (about 15 minutes)

Section A: Picture Conversation (about 5 minutes)

Ask candidates to look at one of the photographs shown below. The first is number 9 and the second number 10 among the Interview Exercises at the back of the Student's Book. Each candidate is assessed for **fluency** and **grammatical accuracy** according to the scales shown on page 12.

9

What's happening in the picture?
What kind of people are they?
Why aren't they sheltering like everyone else, do you think?
Where do you think the photo was taken?

The conversation should lead on to an informal discussion of one or more of the following subjects:

Weather and climate; seasons; friendship.

Questions like the following may help to lead the conversation in the right direction:

How does the weather affect your moods?
What kind of weather do you prefer?
What kind of weather is typical of your country at different times of the year?
What's your favourite time of year?
Can you be 'good friends' with someone much older or younger than yourself?
What are the qualities of a good friend?

10

What's happening in the picture?
What kind of people are they?
Why do you think the young man has *two* trophies?
How do you think both the people feel?

The conversation should lead on to an informal discussion of one or more of the following subjects:

Sports; winning and losing; personal relationships.

Questions like the following may help to lead the conversation in the right direction:

Have you ever won a sporting trophy?
Do you enjoy competition in games or do you play more for enjoyment?
How do you feel if you come first in a competition or school test?
How do you feel if you come last!?
What kind of people do you get on with best?
Describe your ideal romantic partner.

Section B: Reading Passage (about 3 minutes)

Ask candidates to look at reading passage 19 or 20 among the Interview Exercises at the back of the Student's Book. Ask candidates to identify the source and subject matter of the passage before they read it aloud.

19   In the wake of the civil disturbances in some of our inner city areas last year, attention has been given to the roles which national financial institutions and central and local government authorities might play in programmes designed to arrest the economic decay of such areas. We have taken an active role in a number of bodies which are working in areas of immediate concern.

20   He was a very nice man. I think the art is in total contradiction to the character of the man, because the art is really nasty. All those thorns and everything: it's all prickly, all persecuted, all conceived as disagreeable... I never thought the portraits very honest. I'm not at all sure that all those toads and beetles weren't the most natural expression of his interest in life. He didn't care for human beings at all.

Each candidate's **pronunciation** and **stress and rhythm** are assessed according to the scales on page 12.

Section C: Structured Communication Activity (about 5 minutes)

In this section, each candidate's **vocabulary** and **communicative ability** are assessed according to the scales on page 13.

First Communication Activity
Candidate A should look at Interview Exercise 27, candidate B at 35 and candidate C at 43. (Candidate C may be omitted if necessary.)
   Each candidate has a short news report which he or she must paraphrase to the others. Each report has implications which provide material for discussion.
   Allow a minute or two for preparation and then ask each candidate to tell the others about the report in his or her own words. Encourage them to comment on the implications of each story and to criticise the people involved in each. Comments may be made about the following points:

Teacher stabbed: cheating in exams; over-reaction to events; suitable punishment for the accused (or for the teacher?)

Hostess robbed: abuse of hospitality; suspicion of strangers; looking after valuables; suspended sentences

Finding and keeping: public employees' responsibilities; whose word do you believe; what would you have done in the same situation?

Second Communication Activity
Candidate A should look at Interview Exercise 30, candidate B at 38 and candidate C at 46.
   In this activity each candidate has different information about two hotels and the places

they are in. The idea of the activity is that by sharing this information they build up an idea of the attractions and drawbacks of each and then discuss which of them would suit them best for a week's stay in early summer.

If there is insufficient material to sustain the discussion, ask the candidates to describe their 'ideal hotel' and perhaps to talk about some awful hotels they have stayed at or heard about. Candidates with no experience of hotels might be asked to discuss the advantages and drawbacks of different kinds of holidays: staying with family or friends, self-catering, camping, youth hostelling, working holidays, study holidays, activity holidays, etc.

Third Communication Activity (optional reading)

Candidates should look at Interview Exercise 47 for this sample exercise.

47 Have you seen a film or TV version of the text you have read? If so, how did it do justice to the text? What was left out and what needed to be added to make the text into a film? How did the film handle the story and its setting, characters and dialogue?

If you have not seen a film version of the text you have read, what do you think such a film would be like? What would have to be left out or added to make it into a film? Could such a film do justice to the story and its setting, characters and dialogue?

Allow one to two minutes preparation time before asking each candidate to make a statement of his or her views. Then invite candidates to comment on each other's contributions before a general discussion develops. If there is insufficient material to sustain the discussion, ask candidates to comment on film versions of other works of literature, perhaps in their own language, which they have seen.